What People Are

Thoughts are the first step of cre
direct our actions, which direct our future—**Raymon Grace**, President and CEO
of Raymon Grace Foundation, www.raymongrace.us

A unique and approachable way to reprogram the hidden blocks that keep you
from having the life you want—**Jennifer Newcomb Marine**, author of *No One's
a Bitch: A Ten-Step Plan for Mothers and Stepmothers*

A must-read manual on how to get from where you are to where you'd like to be
in your own life. Great philosophy with easy to follow steps to get you on your
way—**Sharón Lynn Wyeth**, author of *Know the Name: Know the Person*

Set yourself free with this potent transformational book! *Claim Your Life* is the
clearest, most down-to-earth, "fill-in-the-blanks" self-empowerment book I have
ever read. Every adult can understand it and do it. Live the life you love now!"—
Ellena Lynn Lieberman, spiritual educator specializing in the Akashic Records,
and author of *The Principles of Dynamic Manifestation: As Received Through the
Akashic Records*, www.dynamicmanifestation.com

When I read and apply *Claim Your Life* easy and simple techniques into my life,
I find that life gets easier and more fun. It is an amazingly easy approach for
fantastic results in a beautiful way so come let's play gongs!—**Faye Henry**, Gong
Player www.tsvibrations.com

Claim Your Life has clarified a way for a person wanting something better to be
able to get inside the hidden places, shed light on dark areas and then actually
transform this non-beneficial energy into powerful, usable life force energy.—
Glenda Garber, Life & Spiritual Awakener – Trainings and personal sessions

We can talk all day, or even for many days, about various paths to a place of daily
love, peace, and joy, about letting go of our old "stuff" and moving on into better
times, but Boni Oian challenges you to write it down, feel it and think it out, and
take action once you're free of unconscious blocks to really manifest what you
want. So, create your own miracle by not just reading this book, but *doing* this
book. Only good will come of it, I promise.—**Joanne Sprott**, Creativity Coach
and editor http://wordtouch.com

CLAIM YOUR LIFE

Transform Your Unwanted Subconscious
Beliefs Into an Exhilarating Source of Power

Also by Boni Oian

Taking out the Trash: Ridding yourself of hurt and frustration

My Workbook to Create MY Reality from Dreams

CLAIM YOUR LIFE

Transform Your Unwanted Subconscious Beliefs into an Exhilarating Source of Power

Boni Oian CH, CART/C, Emily Sanderson, MA, LPC

Editor
AfterWords Editorial Services
Joanne Sprott
713-252-1945
P.O. Box 40424
Houston, Texas 77240-0424

Illustrator
Matt Kramer, Austin, Texas

Photographs by
Beverly Guhl
ARTISTIC PHOTOGRAPHY
Austin, Texas
www.modelmayhem.com/guhl
512.349.7045 [m] 658-6833 Bev@beverlyguhl.com
www.beverlyguhl.com
"One of the best headshot photographers in the country, if not the world . . ."—ProPhotography

BALBOA
PRESS
A DIVISION OF HAY HOUSE

Balboa Press books may be ordered through booksellers or by contacting:

Balboa Press
A Division of Hay House
1663 Liberty Drive
Bloomington, IN 47403
www.balboapress.com
1-(877) 407-4847

ISBN: 978-1-4525-3865-5 (sc)
ISBN: 978-1-4525-3864-8 (ebk)
Library of Congress Control Number: 2011915133

Because of the dynamic nature of the Internet, any web addresses or links contained in this book may have changed since publication and may no longer be valid. The views expressed in this work are solely those of the author and do not necessarily reflect the views of the publisher, and the publisher hereby disclaims any responsibility for them.

The author of this book does not dispense medical advice or prescribe the use of any technique as a form of treatment for physical, emotional, or medical problems without the advice of a physician, either directly or indirectly. The intent of the author is only to offer information of a general nature to help you in your quest for emotional and spiritual well-being. In the event you use any of the information in this book for yourself, which is your constitutional right, the author and the publisher assume no responsibility for your actions.

Any people depicted in stock imagery provided by Thinkstock are models, and such images are being used for illustrative purposes only.
Certain stock imagery © Thinkstock.

Printed in the United States of America

Balboa Press rev. date: 10/10/2011

My thanks to my daughter, who has taught me everything I know.—Emily

For my Father.—Boni

Epigraph

Follow your Bliss and the universe will open doors for you where there were only walls—Joseph Campbell

Contents

FOREWORD

By Ellena Lynn Lieberman, spiritual educator specializing in the Akashic Records, and author of *The Principles of Dynamic Manifestation As Received Through the Akashic Records,* www.dynamicmanifestation.com

The hero charges into the room, smashing the door into smithereens, and rescues us from impending peril. In the past, he broke through, galloping on his unbridled steed. Perhaps now, the door explodes around him, as he, on a jet propelled Harley Davidson (in a color of your choice) sweeps us up against his weathered, metal-crusted jacket, a shield of protection, to the seat behind him. We hang onto his broad, brazen chest. We are saved, but from what? Where do we go now?

Where is the real "free at last?" Where is that hero, who, as Bette Midler sings it, is "the wind beneath my wings?" Where is the stalwart champion who propels us to soar ever higher, seated in our own hearts? Somehow we all know there is that spirit at our very core. Yet life seems to keep erecting walls, boundaries that toughen us each time and restrain us from flight. We seem to never get back to that center where our lives really take off. Sometimes we don't even know what and how we love anymore.

In *Claim Your Life: Transforming Your Unwanted Subconscious Beliefs into an Exhilarating Source of Power,* we are diligently presented with a plan that leads to true liberation. Each process is grounded in clear, step-by-step language, supporting us to fully own our authentic worth and empowerment. We are rescued by our own loving acknowledgement of each brave move we take to see how we have concealed our mighty spirits from our own view. Ultimate liberation occurs when we forgive anyone who appeared to restrain our lives, as we now see them as people participating in the shell of illusion we created around our own bounded, subconscious beliefs. In these pages, the moments of life-altering choice are given to us, as we prepare to shift onto the runway, lift up and blast into the life of true joy and freedom.

CHAPTER 1

Introduction

Thinking is easy, acting is difficult, and to put one's thoughts
into action is the most difficult thing in the world.
—Johann Wolfgang von Goethe

*Honestly, I've tried countless times to "redefine" my life. I really
want to start living the way I've always wanted to live: I want
to get organized; I want to make time for what I love to do; and I
want to relax and enjoy my interests, hobbies and relationships. I
get all motivated; I do tons of work to "de-stress" and "re-order" my
life and career; and, somehow, it all inevitably goes back to stressful
square one . . .*

*I've tried so many times to find and make healthy relationships,
whether finding new relationships or improving relationships I
already have. I make up my mind to work on myself, to communicate,
to set boundaries, to do everything I think I'm supposed to do . . .
but somehow I still end up feeling unfulfilled and taken for granted.
I can't seem to get anywhere . . . It seems like a loop. I'm left feeling
depleted, lonely, and uncertain that this cycle will ever change for
me . . .*

*I've almost given up on trying to lose weight. It's a heartbreaking
cycle for me. I feel embarrassed. I get motivated, I get a plan, I
work so hard, and then I hit a wall. I either run out of steam or get*

1

knocked on my butt by getting sick, injured, or some crisis coming up—something! I fall back, frustrated and exasperated, and judge myself for failing . . . again . . .

Many of us want to change some aspects of ourselves, our lives, or our relationships. Some of us are simply looking to enhance what we already enjoy in our lives, while some of us are looking for a total overhaul to completely remodel ourselves, our life situations and our relationships. Either way we may truly struggle to achieve the changes we seek due to unconscious beliefs we unknowingly hold about ourselves or about life in general. Without realizing it, deep down we may believe that the life we dream of living is "too much" to expect, that we are not fully worthy, or that life just isn't like that.

Unconscious beliefs are just that, totally unconscious. You don't even know that they are there. They are the internalized voices of generations of outside influences, operating like your own personal programming, and they dictate how you perceive yourself, your life, and the world around you. Some of your unconscious beliefs may be serving you very well, and some of them may not be serving you at all. But, either way, your unconscious beliefs drive your life. They are your eyes, your ears and your every assumption. They tell you what is possible and not possible for you, limiting your freedom, choice and happiness.

These unconscious beliefs then sabotage our efforts to create the changes we seek in our lives because, left hidden, our unconscious beliefs will always reinforce the status quo. If I unconsciously believe that I am unworthy, for whatever reason, then I will unknowingly seek out people and situations that "match" that belief. I will unknowingly surround myself with people and situations that reinforce that I am unworthy. I will unknowingly seek out relationships with others that do not treat me with the level of love, value, or respect that all people deserve, because deep down I don't believe that I deserve that same level. When I encounter people who do show me that I am worthy, I will dismiss those people by thinking they are mistaken, inferior, or have ulterior motives. And, when I get motivated to improve some aspect of my life or relationships, I will encounter great difficulty because I will be unknowingly up against my unconscious belief that I am not worthy of the improvements I seek.

In working the steps of *Claim Your Life*, you will systematically reveal these unconscious beliefs, uncovering them so they can be uprooted and replaced with healthy beliefs that empower you and support the changes you seek. This process will put you in the power seat of your life, ushering you into the ideal life you deserve.

Claim Your Life is brief but intense. It is exactly the information you need, no more and no less. The steps of this process are simple, but they are not always easy. Some soul-searching and consistency will be necessary, but the steps are straightforward and broken down into an easy-to-follow workbook format, complete with exercises and examples to support you every step of the way.

Through clear workbook exercises, *Claim Your Life* will help you master five intensely powerful steps to creating the life you choose:

1. You decide *exactly* and *specifically* what you want.
2. You focus consistently on *experiencing* what you want.
3. You watch for distractions or "blocks" between you and what you want to reveal themselves.
4. When a block comes up, you work the steps to uncover the unproductive belief behind the block.
5. You then uproot and replace your unproductive belief with an empowering belief that supports you having what you want.

The impact of these five steps is profound. Clearly understanding these five steps and *applying* them to your life is the key to unfolding your new reality. Once you begin working these steps, you will find yourself positively glowing with freedom, power, and choice. The process itself is so empowering that you will begin to see every "block" as an opportunity for growth and adventure. Your fulfillment and excitement will grow as you uproot unwanted beliefs and embrace the life you want . . . the life you choose.

CHAPTER 2

Getting Started

*It is by going down into the abyss that we recover the
treasures of life.*—Joseph Campbell

Choosing to Begin

Choosing to begin is very brave. While almost everyone would like to change some aspect of their lives, very few people are willing to attempt it. By your bravery, you also reveal your personal belief that change is possible for you. You accurately hold the healthy belief that you are the key to bringing about change in your life. Your belief that you are capable of changing your life is why you picked up *Claim Your Life* and why you are willing to work these steps.

So we know you believe you are capable of changing your life, but *how much* change do you believe you can create? Do you believe you can make a few small changes? Do you believe you can make any changes you like? What is your threshold for happiness? What is your threshold for love or money or freedom? Have you been limiting yourself to wanting things you believe are "safer" to want? Have you been using your energy to create excuses for why your life cannot be the way you really want?

Think of yourself as being in the middle of a bubble (this is your comfort zone). Everything that is in the bubble with you consists of all of the things and relationships you now have (these are the things you have believed possible for yourself so far). The things you still want are outside your bubble. The steps in this book will teach you how to expand your bubble to include all possibilities.

Just imagine expanding your bubble further and further to include everything you want. Your energy must be focused on the thoughts and things that are outside your bubble in order for your bubble to expand to include absolutely everything you want.

As you imagine expanding your bubble further and further, notice that you may believe some of your "wants" are just outside your current bubble, meaning you believe they are closer to your bubble and therefore more attainable for you. And, notice that you may believe some of your "wants" are "too far out" from your bubble, meaning that you may believe those things are far less attainable for you. *Claim Your Life* will challenge you to accept that all things are attainable for you. That there is nothing that is "too much" or "too hard" or "too expensive," just as you cannot be "too lucky" or "too happy" or "too free." The steps to follow will challenge you to remove your limitations on your own possibilities.

As you gain experience with those steps, you will gain trust in this process. And as you gain trust in this process, you will allow yourself to dream bigger and bigger. You can choose to build your muscle on the things you believe are more attainable first, but just know where this process is going. Once you master applying these steps, get ready for the ride.

Choosing to See Where You Are Now

As in any journey, identifying your starting point is the first step toward navigating to your destination. Unless you know where you are, you will not know if you need to take a left, right or keep moving forward.

In this brief section, you'll be asked to complete a description of your life at the moment for the purpose of getting a "baseline." The idea is to briefly and fearlessly write down what you consider to be the basic facts of your life today, including your significant relationships, roles, possessions, events, and situations. Because this exercise is simply about the facts of your life at the moment, try to leave evaluations out of it and just stick to the facts as you perceive them (Remember, this is just about where you are, not about where you want to go or excuses about why you are here).

It's common to be squeamish about describing your current status because it may seem routine or unflattering, especially if you are very unsatisfied in certain areas of your life. But see your brief description as simply the facts of your life at this moment, no more and no less. It is what it is. And you are brave enough to own the truth of this moment and record it objectively. Then you will simply move forward to the process of creating exactly what you *do* want for yourself.

Exercise: Getting a Baseline

Spend a maximum of 15 or 20 minutes filling in the blanks below. This is designed to be a brief exercise to get a "baseline" for change, not an exercise to over-think. You may find that not all the blanks apply to you, or that you need to "tweak" or add some to fit your situation. Just do your best, and do it from your first gut reaction.

In the end, it will read like a personal and factual description of your life at this moment, warts and all. Here's one example:

Diana's Description

My name is <u>Diana Andrews</u>. I am <u>42 years old</u> and live in <u>San Antonio, Texas</u>.

My primary roles are <u>mother, wife and career counselor</u>.

Most of the time I feel I'm good at <u>my job and my relationships</u>, but I'm not so good at <u>confrontation</u>, and sometimes I thinks it's really hard for me to <u>take full responsibility for my own life and decisions</u>.

I generally feel satisfied with my <u>pastimes</u> and get a lot of enjoyment from <u>my dogs and nature trails</u>.

I feel generally dissatisfied with <u>not earning enough income</u> because I want to <u>feel that freedom and power</u> which makes me think/feel <u>anxious that I will not have that freedom and power</u>.

Overall, I feel <u>insecure</u> with the amount of money I have and I feel <u>insecure</u> about my home. My possessions I enjoy the most are my <u>home and car</u> and the possessions I crave the most are <u>more land, a barn, and travel</u>.

Overall, I feel <u>passionate</u> about my job. My favorite thing about it is <u>watching people grow</u>, and my least favorite things are <u>watching people stagnate and complain</u>.

One of my most important relationships is my relationship with <u>my daughter, Sophie</u>. Overall, I feel <u>increasingly good</u> about this relationship. My favorite things about it are <u>laughing, relaxing and enjoying cooking together</u>, and my least favorite things are <u>feeling I was not fully available to her in much of her earlier life</u>.

Another one of my most important relationships is my relationship with <u>my husband, Neil</u>. Overall, I feel <u>increasingly good and secure</u> about this relationship. My favorite things about it are <u>our connection, attraction and simple relaxing lifestyle</u>, and my least favorite things are <u>our struggles to grow financially</u>.

I sometimes feel hurt or angry about <u>unfulfilling friend and family relationships</u>.

I sometimes feel sad or guilty about <u>procrastinating or being a perfectionist</u>.

I sometimes feel inadequate or fearful about <u>money, career and ownership</u>.

I would love to do more <u>relaxing, enjoying, delegating and accepting</u>.

I would love to think/feel less <u>busy, overwhelmed and anxious</u>.

I would love to think/feel more <u>calm, centered and in control</u>.

I often feel my greatest gifts are <u>poise, communication, fairness, and humor</u>.

I often feel most grateful for <u>my daughter</u> because <u>she inspires me and has taught me so much</u>.

Right now, the top three things I'd like to work on first are: 1) <u>to stop making excuses and hiding from my potential</u>, 2) <u>to stop getting delayed by perfectionism, approval, hesitation and other "wheel-spinning,"</u> 3) <u>to</u>

stop procrastinating trying things and doing things just because I don't feel "ready" because I may never feel ready.

Your Turn

My name is _____. I am _____ years old and live in _____.

My primary roles are _____.

Most of the time I feel I'm good at _____, but I'm not so good at _____, and sometimes I thinks it's really hard for me to _____ _____.

I generally feel satisfied with _____and get a lot of enjoyment from _____ _____.

I feel generally dissatisfied with _____ because I _____, which makes me think/feel _____ _____.

Overall, I feel _____ with the amount of money I have and I feel _____ about my home. The possessions I enjoy the most are my _____ and the possessions I crave the most are _____ _____.

Overall, I feel _____ about my job. My favorite things about it are _____, and my least favorite things are _____.

One of my most important relationships is my relationship with my _____ _____. Overall, I feel _____ about this relationship. My favorite things about it are _____ _____, and my least favorite things

are _____
_____.

Another one of my most important relationships is my relationship with my
_____. Overall, I feel _____
about this relationship. My favorite things about it are _____
_____, and my least favorite
things are _____.

I sometimes feel hurt or angry about _____.

I sometimes feel sad or guilty about _____.

I sometimes feel inadequate or fearful about _____.

I would love to do less _____.

I would love to do more _____.

I would love to think/feel less _____.

I would love to think/feel more _____.

I often feel my greatest gifts are _____
_____.

I often feel most grateful for _____
because _____.

Right now, the top three things I'd like to work on first are:

_____
_____
_____

Pit-Stop

Now acknowledge yourself immediately for completing the above task. You have been sincere, brave and truthful in this moment. You are choosing to trust the process. Take a moment to:

1) Write one acknowledgement statement to yourself.
2) Write one encouragement statement to yourself.

Example

1) Acknowledgement: I acknowledge myself for being humble and teachable enough in this moment to complete the above task.
2) Encouragement: I know I can use my strengths to move forward in this process and choose or re-choose whatever I like in my life.

Your Turn

1) Acknowledgment:_____
_____.
2) Encouragement: _____
_____.

Chapter 3

So What Do You Want?

To map out a course of action and follow it to an end requires courage.—Ralph Waldo Emerson

Choosing What You Want

The truth is many of us don't really know what we want. Sometimes we only know that we don't want "this" anymore. Sometimes we only know that we want a "better" job or relationship but don't narrow down the specific attributes that would make our job or relationship better. Not being clear about what we want, specifically, has kept us from getting it. Of course you don't get what you want when you don't even know what it is!

The goal of this section is to identify a clear and specific list of what you want in your life. We will explain this crucial section clearly and provide several exercises and examples because this will give you the clarity and momentum necessary to create the life you crave.

Clarity means you are definite and certain about what you want in your life. When you are clear on the truth of precisely what you want, then you can declare that truth to yourself and the universe. This is setting your intention. Then the momentum begins to bring you and what you want together.

The problem that happens with many of us is that we unknowingly spend our energy focusing on what we don't want. And this will simply never work because the universe, and your subconscious mind, does not recognize the word "not." If you decide that you "do not want to be so stressed anymore," you have just set the intention to continue to be so

11

stressed. You must use positive statements to set intentions, such as deciding "to feel peaceful within myself throughout the day." Your energy must be focused on what you *do* want in order to see it manifest.

So what do you want?

For the purposes of this step, you will be required to believe you can have anything you want. If you find that daunting, you can simply pretend to believe this truth for now until you come to fully believe.

There are three different exercises below designed to help you begin to identify specifically what you want. These exercises can be fun to play with to discover more about yourself and what you really value. The goal is just to come up with a working list of specific "wants" that are phrased in a positive way, communicating what you *do* want. Also, try to use descriptive words; for example, when you say "I want a new job" or "I want to get married," chances are you don't just want *any* new job or *any* marriage, so describe the kind you do want specifically, and use words that feel right to you.

Exercise 1: Translate the "Don't Wants"

It is often easier to list many of your "don't wants" first and then go back and change them into "do wants." Make a list of all the things you don't want in the left column, and then translate the "don't want" statements into what that means you do want. Think of this initial list as a rough draft that will be fun to revise many times for clarity and priority.

Examples from Diana's Story

Don't Want . . .	Do Want . . .
To keep making excuses and hiding from my own potential	To enjoy my power and choice
To be spinning my wheels with perfectionism, approval, and hesitation	To feel efficient and accomplished
To procrastinate trying things or doing things just because I don't feel "ready" because I may never feel ready	To feel empowered to try new things because trial and error is a part of the full and rich life I crave

Other Examples

To feel frustrated and resentful toward my husband for not listening to me or helping me with anything

To feel deeply fulfilled in a love partnership where I feel heard, seen and supported

To feel stressed by car, house and credit card debts which drain me

To feel the peace and security of real financial freedom

To dread going to my stupid job everyday with a boss I can't stand

To love my fulfilling career utilizing my gifts in a healthy environment

To feel obligated, overwhelmed and resentful about my every-day life

To feel lucky to be living my life for real, where I'm empowered to surround myself with what I want

To finally stop feeling so angry and competitive because it just eats me up inside

To feel 100% acceptance and appreciation of myself and others

To stop with the "what ifs" and "if onlys" that seem to clutter my brain and paralyze me from actually doing anything

To feel certain in my decisions and my actions as I complete the tasks I choose

To let go of this aching regret and guilt from my past

To move forward in perfect peace and freedom

Your Turn

<u>Don't Want . . .</u>   <u>Do Want . . .</u>

------------------------   ------------------------
------------------------   ------------------------
------------------------   ------------------------
------------------------   ------------------------
------------------------   ------------------------
------------------------   ------------------------
------------------------   ------------------------
------------------------   ------------------------
------------------------   ------------------------
------------------------   ------------------------

Exercise 2: Do Some "Detective" Work

We can often learn more about ourselves and what we want by noticing our preferred pastimes, habits and surroundings. It can also be helpful to notice those qualities we admire in other people, places and things. This "detective" work can help you identify what you value most and, therefore, what you will want to bring into your life for optimal happiness.

Be your own detective and fill in the blanks below, keeping in mind that you can add, modify or omit whatever blanks you wish. The goal is just to get a "nutshell" version of your likes, dislikes, preferences, etc., which will make it easier to see "themes" in what you want and value.

Emily's Example

One of my favorite activities is <u>yoga</u>, because <u>it makes me feel healthy, powerful and beautiful</u>.

One of my favorite ways to spend a day is <u>hanging around the house, listening to music, drinking tea, and doing art projects with my family because I love relaxing, being connected with Mia, Ali, and kitties, and being creative—so doing it all together is the perfect day</u>.

One of my favorite places in my house is <u>my red chair</u> because <u>it is comfortable and functional, has a view of everything inside and outside</u>.

One of my favorite places in the world is <u>an empty but gorgeous beach</u> because <u>I can relax and walk in beauty and nature and sound</u>.

One of the people I admire most is <u>Boni Oian</u> because I perceive him/ her to be <u>centered, powerful, peaceful and happy, plus she is a successful entrepreneur</u>.

Another person I admire greatly is <u>Stacy Davenport</u> because I perceive him/ her to be <u>centered, powerful, peaceful and happy, plus she is a successful entrepreneur</u>.

If I could meet any famous person I would choose <u>Oprah Winfrey</u> because I value his/her <u>centeredness, power, and positive energy</u>.

If I could speak to any historical figure I would choose <u>Joseph Campbell</u> because I value <u>his expansive and poetic perspective</u>.

One of my favorite movies is <u>*A Beautiful Mind*</u> because <u>it exemplifies how real everything is in our own minds</u>.

One of my favorite books is <u>*Cry, the Beloved Country*</u> because <u>its language is often beautiful and deep, full of journey, redemption and peace (and I love that it takes place in Africa)</u>.

When I was a kid, I wanted to be <u>a vet, home designer or counselor</u> when I grew up because <u>I value animals, beauty, and connection to others</u>.

I have always wanted to travel to <u>Africa</u> because I <u>imagine places that are spacious and rugged and gorgeous</u>.

Someday I am going to treat myself to <u>building my dream house</u> because <u>I've always wanted to build a creative, cozy, low-maintenance family home designed with nature and spaciousness in mind, for art, exercise, and animals and togetherness</u>.

Before I die, I would really love to live <u>a full, simple, and happy life with my daughter and husband (with animals and nature)</u> because <u>I have always wanted to enjoy that together as a family</u>.

I would enjoy being complimented for <u>my poise, my strength, and my good intentions</u> because that would make me think/feel <u>understood and appreciated</u>.

One of my favorite memories is <u>delivering my daughter at her birth</u> because <u>I value intense one-in-a-lifetime moments that require me to rise to the challenge</u>.

A few of my most favorite things in my life are: <u>my family, my cats, my exercise classes and my home by the creek</u> because <u>I value close connection with myself, others, and nature</u>.

If I were not afraid of anything, I would <u>live in perfect faith</u>.

Your Turn

One of my favorite activities is _____ because I feel _____.

One of my favorite ways to spend a day is _____ because _____.

One of my favorite places in my house is _____ because _____.

One of my favorite places in the world is _____ because _____.

One of the people I admire most is _____ because I perceive he/she to be _____.

Another person I admire greatly is _____ _____ because I perceive him/her to be _____ _____.

If I could meet any famous person I would choose _____ because I value his/her _____ _____.

If I could speak to any historical figure I would chose_____
because I value his/her_____
_____.

One of my favorite movies is _____
because _____
_____.

One of my favorite books is _____
because _____
_____.

When I was a kid, I wanted to be a _____
when I grew up because I valued _____
_____.

I have always wanted to travel to _____
because _____
_____.

Someday I am going to treat myself to _____
because _____
_____.

Before I die, I would really love to _____
because_____.

I would enjoy being complimented for my _____
because that would make me think/feel _____
_____.

One of my favorite memories is_____
because_____.

A few of my most favorite things in my life are:_____
because I value _____
_____.

If I were not afraid of anything, I would try _____
_____.

If I were not afraid of anything, I would _____
_____.

Exercise 3: Ranking Your Values

We all have the same values, but we each rank values in a different order. For example, we all value safety and honesty. But if safety is my number one value, and honesty is your number one value, then our decisions and actions in a given situation may be very different (e.g., if we were both held up in a robbery, I may lie to guard my safety and you may tell the truth and choose to fight or run). Knowing we each hold values in a different order can help us understand ourselves and others much better and explain why we differ in decision making, actions and reactions.

Rank the values listed below to see how you prioritize values. Start by at least indentifying the top 10 values that are most important to you, then you can continue ranking more if you'd like. For most of us, our top 5 or 10 values really reveal the "big picture" or framework of who we are and who we want to be, which dictates how we make decisions and take action.

Achievement
Adventure
Ambition
Assertiveness
Awareness
Beauty
Being the Best
Belonging
Centeredness
Certainty
Charity
Chastity
Clarity
Cleanliness
Commitment
Compassion

Consistency
Control
Courage
Creativity
Dependability
Depth
Determination
Diligence
Discipline
Duty
Education
Enjoyment
Excellence
Excitement
Expertise
Fairness
Faith
Fame
Family
Freedom
Friendship
Frugality
Fun
Generosity
Gratitude
Happiness
Health
Honesty
Humility
Humor
Independence
Integrity
Intelligence
Intimacy
Intuition
Justice
Kindness
Leadership

Lineage
Logic
Love
Loyalty
Making a difference
Modesty
Nature
Open-mindedness
Order
Passion
Peace
Poise
Popularity
Power
Practicality
Privacy
Relaxation
Reliability
Resourcefulness
Respect
Sacredness
Sacrifice
Security
Self-control
Selflessness
Sexuality
Simplicity
Solitude
Spirituality
Trust
Victory
Wealth

Refining What You Want

Now that you are getting a lot of ideas, start drafting a list of the things you want in your life. Then work to narrow the list down to your top 10 "wants," and set aside your longer list of ideas for later. It may be hard to decide on just 10 since you've been on a roll, but think of your top 10 as a manageable list to start with, always open to revisions later. (It's fine for you to have less than 10 items, just no more than 10 or else it will be too many to focus on at one time).

Here are further tips on crafting an optimal top 10 list:

- Write your "wants" as if they have already happened and you are enjoying the final results. For example, if you weigh 175 pounds and want to lose 25 pounds, don't write "I want to lose 25 pounds," instead write something like "I feel fantastic weighing 150 and fitting into my beautiful new dress." Picture enjoying your end result and describe it in your own words, experiencing it as something you have attained or accomplished.

- Try to write your "wants" in terms of end results, which is what you really want as opposed to what you believe you must have in order to get what you want. For example, if the only reason you want a new job is because you want more money, then let go of the "how" and just state that you want the money. And most of us don't really want money just to have money, we usually want what we imagine we could do with the money (e.g., pay off my house, retire, travel), so declare your intention for those things instead, believing that they may come to you in varied and unexpected ways.

- Ask for specifics as much as possible, especially regarding money. Rather than writing "lots of money in a secure savings account," write down "$250,000 in a secure savings account," using whatever amounts and words feel right for you.

- Try to breakdown any compound "wants" like "living and working in San Francisco" to be two separate items on your top 10 list, because relocating to San Francisco and getting a job in San Francisco are really two separate things.

- Consolidate very similar or interdependent items if you are having trouble narrowing down to 10; for example, you can consolidate "being happy and healthy" because they can be seen as similar and interdependent in the big picture of your overall wellness. Or you can consolidate feelings you'd like to have about your life or lifestyle, such as "feeling beautiful, peaceful, and powerful every day, inside and out" because these feelings are all under the larger umbrella of your desired self-esteem or self-image.

- And, lastly, just a reminder to add specific descriptions to refine what you want. Again, you do not want just any new job or new love interest, you want one that meets your specific needs and wants so that you can be fulfilled in the new career or relationship. Select words and specific qualities that resonate with you and paint that picture of fulfillment for you.

Your Top 10 List

1. _____
2. _____
3. _____
4. _____
5. _____
6. _____
7. _____
8. _____
9. _____
10. _____

Pit-Stop

Now acknowledge yourself immediately for completing the above task. Most people never take the time to explore and identify what they *do* want. Rather than focus on complaints or excuses, you have worked hard to discover and describe exactly the life you want for yourself. You have declared to yourself and the universe exactly what your mission is, and that is the first step toward fulfilling it.

You have completed a huge step in this process, a step very few people ever take. Take a moment to:

1) Write one acknowledgement statement to yourself.
2) Write one encouragement statement to yourself.

Example

1) Acknowledgement: I acknowledge myself for rising to the challenge of discovering exactly who I am and what I want in this moment.
2) Encouragement: I am excited to move forward with this clarity and create exactly the life I want for myself and my family.

Your Turn

1) Acknowledgment:_____.
2) Encouragement:_____.

CHAPTER 4

Experiencing What You Want

Hold a picture of yourself long and steadily enough in your mind's eye, and you will be drawn toward it—Napolean Hill

Choosing to Experience What You Want

Now that you know what you want, it's time to start living in it. You will begin to focus on *experiencing* what you want right here in the present moment. Since your "wants" are phrased as though you already enjoy having them, you read each item and spend time fully visualizing yourself enjoying the item. What it looks like to enjoy having it, and, especially, what it *feels* like to enjoy having it. These visualizations should include as many of the senses as possible (sight, sound, touch, scent and taste), and be highly personalized to your interests and preferences.

For example, if I desire to be happy and healthy, I don't just read those words off my list, I really visualize the whole picture of what that looks and feels like to me. I picture myself smiling and laughing, full of energy and vibrancy. I picture myself striding confidently out of yoga class and into my home for a healthy snack. I see myself with glowing skin, a strong body and a peaceful mind. I hear the music from my yoga class, I smell the citrus from my healthy snack, and I can feel that my whole being is strong, radiant and blissful.

Your vision of being happy and healthy may be a completely different picture, full of your preferred activities, images, and feelings. The goal is just to create your own unique visualization to allow you to really *experience* having and enjoying what you want, right here in the present moment.

Exercise

Practice *experiencing* what you want

Select one item off your top 10 list to experiment with for this exercise. Now take the item you singled out and decide that you are really willing to have this. Decide that if someone offered it to you today, you would say "Great, thank you!"

Now, first, write the item down on the blank below just as you have written on your list.

Emily's example: <u>I love my deep, close and fun relationship with my daughter, Mia.</u>

Your list item:_____

_____

Now, let's take that item and bring it to life—to your life. Spend a few minutes creating your ideal experience of enjoying this item, relationship or situation. If it is a material item like a house or car, picture the item from at least three different angles so you have a 360-degree view of it. Picture what you would enjoy doing with it, what would it feel like to touch it, taste it or smell it. If it is a relationship, picture the multiple aspects of the relationship such as the closeness, the harmony and the mutual respect. Think of what that would look and feel like: What types of activities would you do? How would you feel inside? Make it as vivid as possible in your mind's eye including your senses and emotions.

Now vividly describe your experience of having and enjoying your item.

Emily's Example

Mia and I are sprawled out on the floor in the living room watching *America's Funniest Videos* together. We are cracking up laughing at the comical videos, and I can feel my belly sore from laughter. I can smell and taste the popcorn we are eating (and we throw a few pieces for our cats to eat, too). During the commercials we talk and laugh and play with the cats. We look at each other laughing, and it makes us laugh even more. I hear her unique cackling laugh, and it makes me feel so happy and grateful to be close to her and enjoy her company.

Your experience having and enjoying your item now:

_____

_____

_____

_____

_____

_____

Now spend some time visualizing enjoying the other items on your top 10 list. It may be helpful to write down full descriptions like you did above, or you may just jot down "trigger" words to help you recall your detailed mental picture. The goal is just to capture your experience of having and enjoying each item, using scenarios and details that are unique and meaningful to you.

1. Item:

   Experience enjoying the item:

2. Item:

   Experience enjoying the item:

3. Item:

   Experience enjoying the item:

4. Item:

   Experience enjoying the item:

5. Item:

   Experience enjoying the item:

6. Item:

   Experience enjoying the item:

7. Item:

   Experience enjoying the item:

8. Item:

   Experience enjoying the item:

9. Item:

Experience enjoying the item:

10. Item:

Experience enjoying the item:

Choosing to Experience What You Want Every Day

Now that you have created a top 10 list of exactly what you want, and how you experience having it and enjoying it, it's time to start focusing daily on what you want in order to manifest in your life.

Daily Focus

Spend 15 minutes every morning and every evening focusing on it. Read each item and really *feel* what it feels like to have it and enjoy it now, taking your time and moving through each of the items individually. You may want to put on relaxing music that is 15 minutes long or set a timer so you don't feel the need to check the time.

While focusing on each item, breathe as deeply as possible. When you breathe you clear your cellular memory, so breathe deeply and exhale deeply. Remember to experience having the item as fully and vividly as possible, incorporating your senses and emotions. If distracting or negative thoughts arise, just notice them and let them pass through, gently redirecting your focus back to experiencing what you want.

TIP #1: Doing your evening visualization right before sleeping can be particularly effective because your visualization then "plays" all night, helping to reprogram your subconscious as you sleep each night.

TIP #2: It can be helpful to come up with a "short-cut" visualization that combines multiple important aspects of what you want so you can quickly put yourself in that positive place in times of stress, or throughout the day as you find extra time. For example, create a vivid "snapshot" of your ideal life, maybe a scene in your ideal home that highlights your abundant lifestyle, positive relationships, and enjoyable possessions. For example, if I desire health, wealth, and fun with close family and friends, I can visualize a fun dinner scene in our beautiful home, with everyone talking and laughing because we all feel so good. I see us all around the table, hear the laughter and chatting, smell and taste the amazing food, and see and feel the beauty and positive energy in the room. This "snapshot" experience can quickly remind me of the overall theme of what I want, relaxing me in times of stress and guiding me in my everyday decisions.

Visualizing what you want, in a vivid and personalized way, allows you to truly *experience* what you want in the present moment, complete with emotions and sensations. You cannot help but smile when you are in the energy of experiencing what you want. You are seeing it, feeling it, and enjoying it—you are living it! And living it internally paves the way for you to live it externally. Dedicating time each day to being in that energy will reprogram your comfort zone (your subconscious) to allow for your desired items and relationships.

Remember, your current comfort zone contains all the things you currently have in your life (these are all the things you have unconsciously believed possible for yourself or "enough" for yourself until now). As you spend time *experiencing* having your desired items and relationships, they become more familiar and comfortable to you. What once may have seemed like an "over-the-top" thing to want, begins to feel more regular and attainable since you are regularly experiencing having it in your life. You enjoy having it, and you relax into the idea of having it all the time, expecting it to be part of your life.

You may begin to notice you lose interest in things in your life that do not align with your vision of what you want. You may notice you just naturally make decisions differently because you are operating from a different perspective, that of your vision. You may notice that all sorts of things and people fall into and out of your life as you and your vision integrate into one. We say "notice" your habits or circumstances in your life changing, rather than "trying" or "making" them change because when you reprogram your subconscious to support what you want, those unproductive habits or circumstances seem to just fade away. You are simply a new person—or, to be more accurate, you are simply the *real* you, without the former distractions, disruptions or baggage.

So how do I reprogram my subconscious to support what I want?

Well, of course, your subconscious does support some of what you want, maybe even quite well in some cases. As we mentioned, you are reading this book now due to your healthy belief that you are the key to changing your own life. But, you now want your subconscious to support everything you want. You want to live optimally, enjoying all aspects of your life to the highest level. To reprogram your subconscious to support this, you must:

1) Focus daily on *experiencing* what you want
2) Detect and clear any "blocks" that come up between you and what you want

Detecting and clearing blocks is the crucial part of reprogramming your subconscious to support everything you want in your life now. "Blocks" are unconscious beliefs disguised as some kind of crisis, and we call them blocks because they stand between us and what we want. A block could take the form of a low-level crisis of "something just came up" like an unexpected work project, the flu, or someone close to you "making" you mad or "needing" a favor. Or a block could take the form of something more serious like a car accident, a panic attack, a serious problem with a loved one, or worse. Sometimes a block can even take form of a "funk" where you feel paralyzed by procrastination, depression, worry, or perfectionism. Whatever the case, the block comes up shortly after you decide to do something new that does not "match" with your unconscious beliefs about what is possible for you.

What usually happens is that you become very upset by the block, get emotional, lose focus and forget all about what you wanted because you are so distracted by the block. Now all your energy and focus is going toward the block (toward what you do *not* want), and little or no energy and focus is going toward what you *do* want. This, of course, doesn't work. You end up giving up on what you wanted and just dealing with the block. At this point the block has served its purpose of reinforcing your subconscious' status quo—you're life is back to the same, back to square one, back to what your subconscious is programmed to recognize as your comfort zone.

Now, are you saying my subconscious can cause illness and accidents, even for others?

No, not necessarily. We are not saying that *every* crisis or unexpected event that blocks you from your goal stems *solely* from your unconscious beliefs. However, what we are saying is that your unconscious beliefs are telling you, "Since this block happened, you can't have or do what you wanted to do anymore," and *you are believing that*. Unknowingly, you are buying into your subconscious' interpretation of the facts: I can't go anymore because my car broke down, I can't start my own business anymore because my mom has cancer, I can't ask for what I want in my relationship because my spouse just blew up and now refuses to speak to me.

We use the block as an excuse to reinforce that we cannot have what we want.

While it may be true that you run into a delay or need to rework your plan, unconscious beliefs cause you to totally lose sight of what you wanted and scrap the whole thing. Essentially, your subconscious will provide endless excuses why your life needs to stay the way it is, and these excuses will be very believable to you if you do not see them as manifestations of your unconscious beliefs.

Here's an example of a typical sequence:

1. **Unconscious Belief**
   I unknowingly hold the unconscious belief that I am not worthy of having a better job.

2. **Desire for Change**
   I notice some of my friends have great jobs that they find fulfilling. I decide that I'm sick of being frustrated with my job and I decide I'm going to get a new job. Using this process, I come up with the specifics of exactly what kind of job I want, and I begin to focus daily on experiencing my dream job where I feel valued and respected. Now the magnet on me and the magnet on my dream job begin to pull together. In order for me and my dream job to fully meet together, every block (unconscious belief) between us has to come up for clearing, so that the path between me and my dream job is clear.

3. **Block Comes Up for Clearing**
   Two days after setting my intention and focusing on it daily, I get a very disturbing phone call at work from my boyfriend that turns into a huge fight. I'm so hurt, angry and confused that I get lost in reacting and the fight escalates into a break-up. Now I have

forgotten all about my dream job because I'm so distracted by the bad break-up with my boyfriend. I have no energy to focus daily on what I want. I have no energy to follow up on any job leads that may have come my way, because I'm in the middle of preparing to move out of his house.

4. **Status Quo: Unconscious Belief is Supported**
So now I go to my same old job every day and feel bad about it. My unconscious belief is reinforced: I do not have my dream job because I am not worthy of having my dream job.

In time, the whole cycle may repeat again. After a period of "normalcy," I may again focus on getting a more fulfilling job, and I will contend with the same block again and again until it is uprooted and replaced.

So is my subconscious just mean or what?

No, your subconscious is not *mean* or out to get you; your subconscious and its unconscious beliefs are just your default programming. Each one of us has unknowingly internalized generations of influences and unconsciously come to conclusions about ourselves, our expectations and our possibilities, which we collectively call our programming or our comfort zone. Even if we don't really like our comfort zone, it's comfortable because it's all we know. It's the part of each of us that says "it's good enough" and "it could be worse" and "life isn't fair." So your subconscious is just trying to do what it has been programmed to think is best for you. It's just trying to keep you "safe" within your comfort zone.

In many cases your subconscious may have served you very well in the past. Your unconscious belief that you should be a "wallflower" may have kept you safe from an abusive parent when you were a child, but now you become frustrated when your spouse or boss doesn't seem to listen to you at all. It just no longer serves who you are and what you want today.

For most of us, the goal of creating our lives or living optimally is a stretch for our subconscious. Certainly some changes we seek may fit comfortably within our current unconscious beliefs, but many significant changes we seek will not. To reprogram your subconscious to support everything you want some unconscious beliefs will have to be uprooted and replaced.

But an unconscious belief cannot be uprooted and replaced if it is not detected. And that is the problem with unconscious beliefs: they hide . . . and they hide very well. Intuitively, we know this because this has been what we've been up against all this time. We tried to make some of these changes before and "something" always got in the way, "somehow" it never quite happened. This is because we unknowingly allowed a block to steal our focus. Then all our attention was on what we did *not* want, instead of on what we did want for ourselves. And, because we didn't realize it was a block, we didn't know to investigate the unconscious belief behind the block, so that we could uproot it and replace it.

Now see how differently the last scenario goes when I'm able to focus daily on what I want *and* detect a block as it comes up:

1. **Unconscious Belief**
   I unknowingly hold the unconscious belief that I am not worthy of having a better job.

2. **Desire for Change**
   I notice some of my friends have great jobs that they find fulfilling. I decide that I'm sick of being frustrated with my job and I decide I'm going to get a new job. Using this process, I come up with the specifics of exactly what kind of job I want, and I begin to focus daily on experiencing my dream job where I feel valued and respected. Now the magnet on me and the magnet on my dream job begin to pull together. In order for me and my dream job to fully meet together, every block (unconscious belief) between us has to come up for clearing, so that the path between me and my dream job is clear.

3. **Block Comes Up for Clearing**
   Two days after setting my intention and focusing on it daily, I get a very disturbing phone call at work from my boyfriend that turns into a huge fight. I'm so hurt, angry and confused that I almost get lost in reacting, but then I have a flash of insight, "Could this be a block coming up for clearing?"

4. **Block Detected!**
    I've been on the lookout for unexpected events that would attempt
    to steal my focus, and I am thinking that I just discovered one!
    This detection makes all the difference.

    Now I'm desperately trying to breathe and not get completely
    carried away with the emotional crisis. I love my boyfriend and
    am very upset by what he is saying, yet I recognize that this event
    is an opportunity to clear a block between myself and the life I
    crave. All I can do is make some excuse to get off the phone with
    him: I tell him I'm sorry but I have to get off the phone now and
    that I will talk with him tonight at home. He angrily protests but I
    repeat myself and follow though. After hanging up the phone, I sit
    down, take a deep breath, and try to collect myself. Then I begin
    courageously working through the block clearing steps (detailed in
    next section) to uncover the unconscious belief behind the block,
    which must be uprooted and replaced for me to get what I want.

The telltale sign that you are experiencing a block is that you are hurt,
frustrated, or angry. The hurt, frustration, and anger are like "doorbells"
chiming to us "Here's a block, would you like to keep it or clear it?" And
because we did not know this before, we unconsciously chose to keep the
block and repeat the cycle again and again. Now, we can choose to stop
the cycle. Now we can choose to detect the block and proceed with the
steps to clear it.

Working the steps transforms the unconscious belief into a conscious
belief, empowering you to make conscious choices going forward. You
will no longer be controlled by an intense "knee-jerk" reaction to that
same situation anymore. You will have the freedom to choose your actions
instead of just reacting. This brings a new level of choice, freedom and
power to you and your life.

Of course, dealing with blocks is not usually a one-time thing. One or
more blocks may come up for clearing when you are focused on one goal,
and more blocks may come up for clearing when you are focused on another
goal. Sometimes the unconscious belief behind various different blocks
may even be the same unconscious belief. For example, in the scenario
above, I may clear my "unworthiness" regarding getting my dream job,
but then I may have to clear unworthiness blocks again when it comes to

getting my dream relationship, or even getting my *next* dream job because wanting those additional things makes me have to expand my comfort zone even further.

But no matter how many blocks come up or how many times they come up, they are opportunities for growth that will clear your path to what you really want, and they get easier to contend with as you build experience in noticing them, uprooting them, and replacing them. Soon you will be excitedly looking for them because you know the process will bring you the results you crave.

CHAPTER 5

Clearing Blocks

Everything that irritates us about others can lead us to an
understanding of ourselves.—Carl Gustav Jung

Choosing to Clear Blocks

Again, blocks usually come up shortly after you have decided to do something new. Then, while you are focusing on that new thing, a block comes up to try to steal your focus. This is usually in the form of someone saying or doing something that upsets you, but can also be an event that happens that upsets you. Whatever the form, the block catches your attention and your emotions, and distracts you, leaving you "thrown off" and upset.

Unfortunately, it is easy to forget that what is upsetting you is really showing you a belief about yourself. Forgetting this fact—that it is really about you—makes you very upset with the other people or circumstances involved and keeps you from taking advantage of opportunities to eliminate your unconscious beliefs that are causing you pain.

You have the opportunity to realize and eliminate hurt, frustration and anger in your life by way of "projection." Projection is the name given to the process of your mind "out-picturing" your own beliefs about yourself on to someone else, much like a movie projector. When the mind uses projection, it is like shooting an arrow attached to a string on to someone else. You are now connected to this other person emotionally; therefore you will have a difficult time forgetting this person. Everyone with eyesight in a room can see everyone else directly. The only one you cannot see directly is yourself. You utilize projection, like a mirror, so you can see yourself.

Block Clearing Steps

Step 1: Hurt, Frustration or Anger

Whenever we feel hurt, frustrated or angry then we know we are dealing with a block that has come up for clearing. Our feelings of hurt, frustration and anger are simply the doorbells telling us that there is an unconscious belief underneath those feelings that is no longer serving us. The best way to uncover that unconscious belief is to begin with what triggered those feelings of hurt, frustration or anger.

You can start here anytime your awareness notices triggered feelings, as this step is the most definable. Noticing that you are upset is a clear indication that an unconscious belief is standing between you and the way you want to live.

Exercise

Briefly describe the interaction or event that triggered your feelings of hurt, frustration or anger. If you are not upset about something now, just recall the last time you were upset and investigate that incident.

Question: Who or what do you believe caused you to feel hurt, frustrated or angry?

Example answer: When I was at the grocery store today, a woman let her child ram into me repeatedly with a grocery cart. I told the child to stop and told the woman what was happening, expecting her to discipline her child. However, the child just continued ramming me with the cart and it seemed the woman did not care at all. I'm furious with the woman for allowing her child to ram me continuously and not even attempt to intervene or apologize for the situation.

Your answer:_____

Notice how the emotions come back to you: your confusion, your hurt, your frustration, your anger. Notice your critical thoughts and judgments of the other people or circumstances involved. Clearly, one of your "buttons" has been pushed, making it difficult for you to forget the event. You may find yourself replaying the scene in your head, mentally arguing with the other people in the situation even though they are long gone.

The hurt, frustration and anger you continue to feel makes you a prime candidate for Step 2, which is an optional step wherein you complain to others about the incident because you do not yet realize it was your own unconscious belief coming up in the form of a block. We say Step 2 is an "optional" step because if you are aware that your hurt, frustration and anger are really due to an unconscious belief you hold, you can skip to Step 4 to uncover the belief. However, it can be very difficult to catch yourself and realize you are dealing with a block, especially initially when your emotions are still intense, so you may have to go through Steps 2 and 3 in order to realize the problem is really your unconscious belief.

Step 2: Whine, Bitch, Moan (optional step)

This step is just what it sounds like: You tell others about the incident, you whine, bitch and moan, and you perhaps even blame others for where you are in your life. As we've said, this step is optional. There are occasions where some "venting" calms you down enough and takes enough time, so that you can then catch yourself and realize this is a block. But there are many times when people can remain stuck in this "Whine, Bitch, Moan" step for long periods of time, never realizing—or at least never admitting—that it is really about them.

The hurt, frustration or anger you feel is signaling an opportunity to clear an unconscious belief that is no longer serving you. If you do not recognize this as an opportunity, your resulting actions are usually a replay of unwanted behavior patterns. Some of the unwanted behavior patterns could be whining, avoiding places where things could happen to you, retreating to a comfort zone, attempting to take control of your environment, looking for self-verification, or even blaming your whole life on someone else.

When you choose to whine, you have a dramatic play ready for production. If this is your pattern, it makes this behavior hard to release because it is so much fun!

You now have a great conversation starter. You can get worked up emotionally, employ all of your acting skills, and find cast members to play and sing along. This adds to your production because you can get an unlimited number of people to join the drama, inviting everyone to feel totally connected and on the same wavelength. You can keep the complaints going for days; replaying the whole scenario over again and again. This is similar to the reruns of the football game or your favorite sitcom.

You can start your own cast party in the lunchroom and have a table reserved for the people who know their parts. The term "clique" has been given to a group such as this. People who have had similar experiences will be attracted to this group. They will also hold similar beliefs.

Eventually all you have to say are the key words to have the play begin. You can drag it home, get your kids and spouse to give you sympathy as a way of getting attention.

When your family is really good at pampering you, you are able to drag out your production for months or even years. This means you do not have to take responsibility for your life, your own choices, or deal with releasing old beliefs.

You can find references from your past as to why this is happening to you, convincing everyone why it will always be this way, and how you are the victim to these villains. You get to make this whole drama someone else's fault.

If you don't have a cast system to support your play, you may choose to quit going places where your hurt, frustration or anger are likely to get triggered. To avoid such encounters you may avoid many of the people in your life, or decide not to meet any new people or try new things. Living in this fear limits your freedom, makes your world smaller, and limits new experiences that would benefit your growth or awareness.

Another popular choice to avoid growth or awareness is to retreat to a comfort zone. People who do this know exactly what this means. Comfort zones vary depending on personal interests. You go to a physically safe place in your home, like your bed, covering up with blankets, or curling up in your favorite chair. You may choose a body comfort like eating chocolate, ice cream, or your favorite meal, or by drinking a soothing beverage.

Also there are distractions that comfort you by helping you escape reality, such as reading a book, watching your favorite movie, taking a nap, crying, or focusing on other people's problems. This behavior pattern is about replaying old patterns where you once felt comfortable, in control, or like your old self.

You could change your hairstyle or hair color, add piercings or tattoos to parts of your body, paint something, rearrange the furniture, or renovate your bedroom in an attempt to control your environment.

Anything that involves action to change what you can about your body or environment allows you to feel in control of your life. This gives you the security that the mind needs to feel that you are in charge of your life. What you are really doing is stuffing your feelings about the situation down deeper or denying that they are there.

To appease the hurt feelings, you may resort to self-verification. You have lots of behavior options to validate that you exist, have value, or are in control of yourself and that you are important in other people's lives.

Some actions could have you dressing provocatively with the intent of turning heads, or walking around a store doing negative acts to be noticed, or bullying someone to feel superior. Shopping just to spend money fits in this category. Shopping to purchase something you do not need just because "you are worth it" can also negatively verify your self-worth.

Once the need to be in control of your life is met and you have convinced yourself that you are valuable or in control of the situation, your life can go back to what seems normal until the issue that pushed your button appears again.

Bobbie's example:

Bobbie is an example of a lady who stays cycling between her normal feelings, getting her buttons pushed, and finally getting back to her normal feelings, which we call an endless loop or repeating pattern.

Bobbie is a beautiful lady and wants to be married.

She works outside the home and is a single mom with three kids still at home. She is always on the lookout for a man to marry.

Bobbie has friends that are married and she thinks it is time to have the relationship she has always dreamed of having and she chooses to have such a relationship.

Bobbie starts by inviting men to her home for dinner.

One of her acquaintances, Dave, takes her invitation for dinner as a wonderful, kind gesture. As the evening progresses he proceeds to spend the evening telling her about his engagement party scheduled for Friday. He invites Bobbie to attend. This brings up hurt feelings in her because her hidden agenda or intention for inviting Dave to dinner was for him to see her as his spouse. This leads to angry feelings on her part.

She whines to others about how Dave's fiancée is taking advantage of his vulnerability. She is convinced the other woman is a manipulating gold digger.

Bobbie goes to the engagement party to upstage the fiancée by dressing seductively; charming everyone by being the life of the party, and making sure everyone knows she was Dave's close and personal friend. This satisfies Bobbie's need to validate that she is still a beautiful woman and a prize for any man.

Better yet her point was made as Dave noticed how beautiful Bobbie looked. This plus Dave's fiancée's reaction of jealous behavior about Dave noticing Bobbie validated her so she could happily glide back to her normal day, temporarily forgetting that she originally wanted a husband.

Until Bobbie sees this inappropriate seduction behavior as an unwanted pattern she uses to validate herself and chooses to break it, she will stay single, enjoying the chase of unavailable men.

Another option Bobbie could choose is to abandon the idea of ever getting married. This typically would only occur if the pain of the behavior outweighs the need for validation.

Only when Bobbie truly believes she really is a wonderful desirable person, deserving of a wonderful relationship with a man complete with the commitment of marriage, will her dream become a reality.

Note: Every time you do any of these actions you are not necessarily repeating old or unwanted behavior patterns. Remember these examples apply only where the behavior patterns are unconscious, *only if the action seems uncontrollable*. This section describes common unconscious or "knee-jerk" behaviors that we do when we get hurt, frustrated or angry, which actually cause us to lose focus on what we want and take us further toward what we don't want. You can certainly consciously choose to try a new hairstyle, rearrange furniture, or even dress seductively if that is enjoyable to you; the idea is not to do these behaviors to avoid a real issue in your life.

Exercise

Reflect on your patterns of unwanted behavior in any of these areas that apply.

List at least three people to whom you whine when you play out your drama.

1)
2)
3)

List three locations/places you have eliminated from your life when your choice is to hide.

1)
2)
3)

List three areas you retreat to if your choice is to retreat to a comfort zone.

1)
2)
3)

List three ways you validate your worth when your choice is self-verification.

1)
2)
3)

Step 3: You or Someone Else Breaks Your Pattern

At some point, you or someone else lets you know it is time to get off the stage or brings it to your attention that your behavior patterns are destructive or not getting you what you want.

You are the only one with yourself all the time so ideally you would be the most likely person to catch the behavior and you are the only one who can change it. You are also the only person to whom you cannot lie. You may be able to suppress the feeling for a while, but deep down you know you are lying to yourself.

Other people may assist you by putting up road blocks in an effort to change your awareness about your behavior in one of two ways:

1) Getting slapped without (g)love or

2) Getting slapped with (g)love.

Without (g)love sounds something like this: "Quit your bellyaching. I'm tired of hearing you play victim, you are such a loser." The result of this approach may cause you to immediately run for a comfort zone or try to defend yourself or your actions. This is not an empowering approach.

The second way, with a (g)love, allows you to be given the choice of removing the block while being aware of the process. It looks like a dance. Standing on the dance floor, you step back so you can see and listen to what is really happening. Stepping back in this case is stepping back emotionally. You tell yourself the truth of the situation by noticing only the facts.

This approach gently stops the behavior in the moment and lets you take stock of your choices and options for further behavior.

Examples of you noticing and breaking the behavior patterns with (g) love are:

- When I jump into bed and pull the blankets over my head, I will immediately get up, move to the desk and write down the facts of what happened in the last 24 hours.
- As soon as I hear myself complaining about what someone did, I will yell "Stop!" and then immediately stop what I am saying and move on to remembering what I really wanted and focus on it in my mind's eye while breathing deeply.

Think of three ways you are willing to break your pattern with (g) love:

1)
2)
3)

List anyone you trust enough to help you through this process. You don't have to do this alone. You can ask a trusted friend to make you aware of when he/she notices you are repeating the same pattern or story. Ask him/her to bring this to your awareness by asking—"Haven't I have heard this story or pattern before?" and then ask if he/she can follow the statement with an example.

The following is another place you can get stuck or stay unaware. The unawareness includes the cycle of having your button pushed where you react with unwanted behavior. Then when someone breaks your pattern, it pushes your button again so you act out more unwanted behavior, and again someone breaks your pattern, etc. This is familiar to many people.

Anita's example:

Anita is a perfect example of someone repeating the endless loop of this process or repeating cycle. She stays in a constant "ticked off" emotional state. It would feel foreign to her to feel at peace with herself or others.

Her normal or typical day starts by going to work.

It's not long before her ex-husband, who is her current employee, does something that upsets her. So she calls someone to complain about his incompetence. At some point in the conversation, the person Anita is talking with does not want to hear any more. The person may attempt to defend Anita's ex-husband, ask Anita to quit complaining, or offer a solution like getting rid of the ex-husband as an employee. Whether or not this is done with compassion or a (g)love, this makes Anita even madder and she finds someone else on which to dump her bitchy behavior.

As soon as this new person stops her from dumping on them, she is mad again.

Her behavior continues all day until "happy hour," where Anita can now complain to a group at the bar and try to get sympathy for the rough day she had and all the crazy people in her life. To Anita this is a normal or typical day. She fails to see the cycle in which she is stuck. She also has forgotten that she too has wanted a harmonious work environment.

The people Anita dump on have mistaken her behavior as a request for a solution to her problem when, in fact, Anita just likes to dump. This allows her to feel superior, lets her continue in her belief that she has the right way to do things, and has to be the watchdog over others. Having something to whine and complain about allows Anita to keep reinforcing this belief that she is right or superior.

Is there any area of your life where you maintain a perpetual cycle like this?

If there may be a cycle like this in your life, and you would like to move out of it, then you are ready for Step 4.

Step 4: Ask Yourself Questions

Remember the incident you described in Step 1 that left you feeling hurt, frustrated, or angry? Now ask yourself these six questions about that incident. These questions will only assist you when you choose to answer them truthfully:

1) What did the actions of the other person make you think about them?

2) What does that tell you about you?

3) How does that relate to how you handle similar situations?

4) How does making them wrong, elevate or serve you?

5) Why am I (*insert answer from question one*)?

6) Who am I (*insert answer from question one*) towards?

Let us review the grocery store incident given as an example in Step 1 and see how these same questions could be answered:

When I was at the grocery store today, a woman let her child ram into me repeatedly with a grocery cart. I told the child to stop and told the woman what was happening, expecting her to discipline her child. However, the child just continued ramming me with the cart, and it seemed the woman did not care at all. I'm furious with the woman for allowing her child to ram me continuously and not even attempt to intervene or apologize for the situation.

1) What did the actions of the other person make you think about them?

   It made me think that she did not have control of her child; she did not care if she had control, and she did not care what the child did to me.

2) What does that tell you about you?

   It tells me that I believe no one cares what happens to me.

3) How does that relate to how you handle similar situations?

   I always end up getting hurt and no one cares.

4) How does making them wrong elevate or serve me?

   Then I do not have to look at why it keeps happening because that might lead back to me. I can stay a victim and don't have to change.

5. Why am I (*insert answer from question one*)?

   From the example: Why am I (not caring what happens to me)? Because I believe I am not worth the trouble.

6. Who am I (*insert answer from question one*) towards?

   Who am I (not caring) towards? Just about everybody, because if no one cares about me I don't have to care about them.

The last part of this statement is how you justify your behavior.

Justifying your behavior is a wonderful way to realize that your behavior is either out of character for you or that you are unwilling to change the behavior.

You don't have to ask yourself all these questions. You may stop as soon as you recognize your situation, belief or block.

So now that I know my belief, what can I do about it?

Realizing that this is about you is the toughest thing you will have to face. The good news is that it is from this place that you have the power to change things.

The hardest parts about this realization are the feelings of shame, guilt and embarrassment that accompany it. Not wanting to feel these feelings is why you are choosing to believe it is about other people instead of about you. It keeps you from facing the truth and keeps it out of your awareness.

When you get to the question of "What does that tell me about them?" you are ready to hear "What does this tell me about me?"

Now that the realization has come home, you know what you have been avoiding.

Let yourself feel the embarrassment, humiliation or humbleness. Take a deep breath. You have come through the hardest part!

Congratulations!

You may want to mark this breakthrough by congratulating yourself with a song or dance.

List three ways you can acknowledge yourself for completing these steps.

1)

2)

3)

Now is the time to see your clear choices.

You can choose to hold on to the delusion that you are a victim of the situation. If you believe that staying a victim of the situation still serves your needs, and it is what you want and how you want to feel, continue the behavior pattern.

By this choice you are choosing to stay invisible about that which you really are—the creator of the situation.

You can pretend that you have no personal power to change anything in your life. By pretending you do not have personal power, you ensure that your life will stay exactly as it has been and it is how you want your life to continue.

When you choose to keep the block submerged and agree that you want to keep your present belief system, you are creating a more powerful belief root system. The next time that block has an opportunity to rise;

it will be under an even deeper layer of experiences that supports your delusion of being the victim instead of the creator.

Once this delusion is chosen, you must recycle back to a lower step so you can stay trapped in the endless loop cycle you have created, thereby stagnating yourself. You cannot go forward into releasing the cause.

On the other hand if you are now ready to move on to changing the belief, you can start to release the block by acknowledging that you created this opportunity for growth and preparing yourself to move forward to the next step.

By choosing to let this irritation surface and deal with the feelings that accompany it, you have taken away the power it had on your life. It can no longer unconsciously have you repeat unwanted behavior patterns.

By allowing the unconscious block to become conscious, you have created choice in one more areas of your life. Let yourself feel how really good that feels.

Which is your choice?

- *To pretend you have no personal power and that you are a victim in the situation (By choosing this you are saying, "My life is exactly how I want it.")*

or

- *To uproot this block and move forward*

Here is how the uprooting happens: Start by being grateful for all the people, places, things, events, and experiences that have contributed to your past behavior. Then forgive everything that led up to this point of time that supported that old belief. Next, acknowledge all the people, places, things, events and experiences that contributed to the awareness of this unwanted behavior. Finally, forgive all involved.

Write your name on the top line of a clean sheet of paper, then list everyone involved in the situation you are analyzing. Make sure you list all of those wonderful people that at a moment's notice jumped into your life to help you play out the scene. Also add to the list everyone you remember who ever played a part in your play, going as far back in your life as you can remember.

Now start thanking all those people. Really be grateful for the assistance and support you received in completing this lesson. Even if you feel you are making up reasons for thanking them, do it anyhow.

Do you remember the lady in the grocery store? With her as an example, we could thank her for being so distracted that she let her child ram you with the cart so your limiting block could be brought to your conscious awareness. This gave you the opportunity to choose to clear that block.

Be grateful for the release of yet another block. This block has been keeping you from enjoying the quality relationships you know you can have in your life. It has been keeping you from the freedom you were given at birth to enjoy every moment of your life.

Forgive yourself for not utilizing this knowledge previously. Sometimes you think you should have known in kindergarten what has taken a lifetime of experiences to learn. You came into this life with the ability to learn each lesson in a sequential manner for the completion of your soul's mission. Sometimes you tend to forget that you needed to have the experiences of grade school through high school, prior to college, so you know how to succeed in college. The same strategy applies in life.

Now forgive yourself for not realizing that the other people were only playing important roles for your opportunity of growth. This removes any guilt you have from what you said or thought before you knew that everyone else was helping you. Use your list of everyone involved and forgive them for how they played their parts.

Appreciate everyone for how they played their roles in this scene by noticing their creative abilities. Notice how realistically they played their parts.

1. *List everyone in the situation.*
2. *Thank everyone listed above.*
3. *Forgive yourself for not knowing this lesson previously.*
4. *Forgive yourself for not knowing everyone was playing a part to help you grow.*
5. *Forgive everyone for how convincingly they played their part.*
6. *Feel grateful that so many people were willing to help you see this part of you.*

Then use one of the forgiveness statements below to wipe the slate clean, to release the story that holds you in place, or keeps you stuck in an unwanted pattern of behavior or unpleasant feelings.

You may choose to create your own forgiveness statement, using words that fit the details of the experience, if that seems more fitting. The idea is simply to express a sweeping and genuine forgiveness statement to fully release the block, thus creating the space to invite in joy, freedom, and conscious choices.

You may choose to use a forgiveness statement every day and every night to clear any misperceptions you may hold that are still affecting your life in a non-empowering way. Even subtle misperceptions can be limiting your choices and thus be limiting your freedom to choose in an area of your life.

Statement of Forgiveness

- I forgive everyone and everything that ever hurt or frustrated me either intentionally or unintentionally. I forgive myself for ever hurting or frustrating anyone intentionally or unintentionally.
- I forgive everyone and everything, including myself, who has ever hurt or frustrated me. Also if I ever hurt or frustrated anyone I forgive myself, throughout all time, space, and all dimensions.
- I totally and completely forgive everyone, including myself, for how each person chose to accomplish his or her role in my life. I accept everyone's choices along with my choice as part of the free will we are all given to express ourselves.

You may also write a letter to each person involved in your story explaining how you see things differently now. When you are finished composing your letter, burn or tear it up instead of mailing it. Burning the letter or tearing it up needs to be done as a ritual of release, not out of anger. The fire symbolizes the transformation of solid, stuck thoughts and feelings into freedom and release. Say "I am now willing to let go of these things that have held me back from living the life I want" as you drop each piece into the fire.

Now refocus on what you want in your life. What was the original picture of what you wanted in your life? Remember the one thing you chose to focus on for this illustration. See those three pictures you envisioned and move into receiving the gift of joy.

Relax and breathe. Take five deep breaths, slowly breathing in and out while acknowledging yourself for completing and eliminating a belief that had kept you from living the life you wanted.

You have now created space by removing the block! The place the unconscious block occupied is now available for joy. This process is automatic, like taking a rock out of the bottom of an aquarium filled with water. Immediately the area the rock occupied is replaced with water. The only difference with the space left by the unconscious block is that joy, instead of water, expands to fill the vacuum. So laugh and let the joy fill up the space you have just cleared! This could be your next humorous story at the office Christmas party. As Phyllis Diller once said, "Humor is tragedy revisited."

List three things that bring joy into your heart:

1)

2)

3)

Then choose to do at least three things that bring your heart joy every day.

Now you know the process of ridding yourself of hurt and frustration so you can exercise the real power you have to create the life you want.

This has taken care of one block in your life; unfortunately we have found we all have many blocks. We are willing to live with some of these blocks for awhile, and other blocks are getting in our way today.

We invite you to use this system of removing blocks as many times as you want to make your life easier and to bring peace, love and joy into everything you do, say and experience.

Watch what happens in your life; make changes and choices as you see how your behavior better aligns with what you want in your life. Remember your anger, irritation, hurt feelings or inconveniences are doorbells to alert you to your blocks along the way. Continue to address these blocks and work through them to learn their lessons; this will clear the way for the lifestyle and relationships you have always wanted for yourself and your family.

CHAPTER 6

Personal Stories

The possibilities are numerous once we decide to act and
not react.—George Bernard Shaw

Personal Stories

The following are examples of how other people came into awareness of their behaviors.

Lorraine's Story

Meet Lorraine. She is married and has a teenage son. She calls herself a domestic goddess as she has few responsibilities in and around the home except for grooming and indulging herself.

Lorraine agreed to allow me to share the story of her recent awareness that came from this process. Initially we started by having her think back to the last time she got mad at someone. She has been doing things her normal way at her house for a while but wanted to change her relationship with her husband.

One day a man showed up at the door and told Lorraine he had been working in the area paving driveways. He had extra blacktop. Instead of trashing it he would pave her driveway for $200 with the blacktop he had left. If she wanted more blacktop it would cost $2 a square foot. Lorraine told him to proceed and to let her see when the first $200 part was finished. The man leveled the driveway and used his leftover blacktop, which covered approximately a quarter of the driveway.

He then told her it would cost $1,800 to finish the driveway. Lorraine became ballistic, no way was she going to have him finish the driveway and told him so.

She called friends and family members totally indignant.

I smiled as she told me the story. This made her laugh because she saw right away what I had explained to her about the steps of the process.

So I proceeded with the following question, "Why did that make you mad?" Lorraine's answer was because the salesman was trying to manipulate her. If the salesman would have stated right up front what the driveway was going to cost, then Lorraine could have made a decision before he started. So I asked, "On whom do you use that same technique whereby you get what you want?"

Before she could think, the words "my husband" spilled from her mouth. She immediately put both hands across her mouth so nothing else would escape. Bingo—she got it. She realized this was a mirror to show her how it felt to be set up and manipulated.

Lorraine got the connection that she created this experience because she wanted tensions to be dissolved between her husband and herself. Lorraine realized she had the power to change things by understanding her choices and picking one. She chose to move forward.

We listed all of the people that played in this performance. This included the obvious people, such as the blacktop man and his crew, and all the people who listened to her complain, including her husband. She expressed gratitude for everyone who came to her aid in order for her to see and experience herself and her actions. Lorraine thanked her mother for teaching her this pattern, plus all the people who had previously tried to demonstrate this lesson. Lorraine even was grateful for all of the people though out the years where her manipulation didn't work, teachers that let her continue her pattern and, of course, herself. Then using that same list, she forgave everyone, starting with herself, for the role each played. Lorraine even acknowledged how masterfully each one had played their part going into detail with theatrics.

Continuing on, we relaxed and breathed, chuckled and giggled. Then Lorraine said, "The one thing that helps me laugh at all this is that I realize everyone clears blocks the same way."

Sally's Story

My friend Sally is an energetic 68-year-old massage therapist.

One day she was daydreaming about having an abundance of money to spend that she had earned from her business, and it really struck her how she would love to be wealthy.

A new therapist started working at the salon where Sally worked. Sally thought this new therapist was the most obnoxious person because this therapist would intrude in conversations between the clients and other therapists. She would race to answer the phone, so that regardless of who the client requested, the new therapist would schedule the client with herself. On top of all of this, the new therapist had the nerve to wear blue jeans, which Sally judged as unprofessional. Sally was willing to look at her anger because she hated how she felt.

Sally hated that she joined in the griping and moaning with the other therapists, which lasted for months. She and the rest of the therapists became a tight group of gossipers. Sally was not happy with herself or the part she was playing, because she prided herself for not participating in putting other people down.

Sally couldn't take it anymore so she made the decision to quit that spa. However, the new therapist got fired before Sally turned in her notice.

When Sally came to me for assistance, we started by stating exactly what it was about the other therapist that pushed Sally's buttons. We came up with a list. When the therapist would offer verbal assistance, Sally thought she was bragging. When the therapist would help out by answering the phone and scheduling clients' appointments, Sally thought the therapist was stealing her clients. When the therapist would dress casually, Sally thought she was unprofessional. This process of fact finding helped Sally separate facts from Sally's opinions.

The bottom line was that Sally knew more about massage than she ever voiced because "she was not brought up that way." Sally didn't answer the phone because she was afraid the other therapists might think she was stealing their clients. Sally wanted the respect given to doctors, so she dressed like one. Her limitations became clear. She had conflict within herself concerning communication when talking about her skills. Sally could not schedule clients for herself without feeling like she was taking a client away from someone else. Sally also believed she was not good enough; so she covered her feelings of inadequacy by acting and dressing like her perception of a respected professional.

Sally was so embarrassed when the realization came to her that she co-created this situation to assist her in recognizing her own unconscious blocks. Sally kept saying "I know I'm not the one causing this person to be in our lives at the meetings that were held about the problem therapist." Now Sally realized it was she who was benefiting from the situation.

It was time to move forward, and yes, Sally could see how this experience was set into motion by wanting to expand her own business and gain recognition for her knowledge.

Sally started being grateful for everyone that was involved in this incident. Plus she forgave herself as well as everyone on her list.

We laughed at how it all had played out; it was such a sitcom drama. She was jumping up and down yelling, "It will be great to be wealthy now!"

Phil's Story

Phil is a wonderful guy, a family man, and a business wizard. Normal life for him is working at the job he loves, being active in his civic group, and promoting spirituality.

At work one day, Phil realized he had the next two weekends planned. He hadn't really been spending much time with his family, which was important to him.

He started fantasizing what it would be like to have time to travel with his wife and kids.

The phone interrupted his thoughts. The call was from his mother. She was on her weekly whining routine about how she did not feel well and how he needed to take better care of her needs. Being totally frustrated and so tired of this endless pattern of her sickly routine, Phil called an ambulance to go get his mom and take her to the hospital.

Phil had called me to confirm a civic function when the story about his mother was shared.

Because Phil and I have an open, honest relationship, I was able to help him break his pattern quickly. It did surprise him that instead of just listening I started asking questions.

The questions went like this: Why do you feel she continually does this sick thing? His answer was, so she could control him. So, why do you feel powerless to say no? Immediately the guard came up and out of his mouth came: "If it were your mother you would feel the same way, do the same thing. Then you would know what it is like." I reminded him we were not talking about my mother. He shared that he felt he did not have control of his time or his life when his mom was sick, and that he had no choice. He slowly realized he did have control, because he chose how much time and energy he spends handling her affairs.

He chose quickly to rid himself of this belief and moved forward, being grateful without even being coached to do so.

Phil started being grateful for his wife who helps out with his mother, his kids for keeping his mother occupied, and his sister for assisting when she is in town. Phil also realized that he'd been doing what he wanted to do all along. He would not really have chosen to spend his time any differently.

With this forgiveness, his joy returned and Phil said he felt a real healing take place.

Two days later, Phil said he didn't know how I did it, but I had even changed his mother! When he went to see her she was nice. She told Phil she was not having the operation, even though only a few days ago she had stated she would die if the operation were not done. His mom then asked Phil his opinion on an assisted living home. When he told her it was her choice because she was the one that had to live there, she said "yes, you're right." He said he had never ever heard her utter those words previously.

Jack's Story

Jack is the most helpful person I know. He's so helpful that many others in our office building take full advantage of his generosity. It reminds me of the saying that there are two kinds of people in the world, those that do and those that let them.

Jack's normal day consists of saying his prayers immediately after waking, watching the *Today Show* while drinking his coffee, choosing between oatmeal and cereal for breakfast, checking the status of his bank account, pressing his clothes, taking a shower, gathering stuff for the day, going to the grocery store, going to the bank, and then arriving at work via the same route. He does the same routine every day except on Thursday.

One of his prayers every morning is to let him be able to "go with the flow."

He has noticed around him that others accept changes so much better than he does.

While talking in the hall with Jack one day, I inquired if anyone ever made him mad. He replied that just 10 minutes ago his cousin had made him really angry. He continued with how she does nothing, does not work and never did. She was 60 years old and had always been dependent on someone else. Jack's cousin, nicknamed the Queen Bee, called him to inquire why Jack had not done her taxes since she thrust the job upon him five days previously. Her call was inspired by the fact that she had made an appointment with the accountant for the following day.

Immediately Jack called some people who knew the Queen Bee. Together they went into the "you know how she is" routine. They completely bonded and aligned with how everything has to be done for the Queen Bee. They laughed and said some things he refused to repeat to me. This reinforced that he was a victim to his relative, and he was right to think about her the way he did.

Jack felt better having vented his frustration and having his friends agree with him, thus he could get back to work.

I asked, "What actually happened?" He answered, "She was telling me what to do and giving me deadlines on doing it."

I asked, "What did that tell you about her?" Jack said, "She thinks she can tell me what to do because I'm a nice guy." I asked, "What does that tell you about you?" Jack said, "I don't like being told what to do because then I am doing something because of expectations instead of volunteering." I asked, "Jack to whom do you tell what to do?" Jack answered, "I tell my girlfriend what to do. I have to be able to boss my girlfriend around to make myself feel better. Then I do not like the fact that she lets me boss her around, so we fight."

Jack said, "I get it now. When others tell me what to do and I do it, I feel mad—really at myself—for letting them boss me around, then I do the same thing to someone else."

Jack then chose to move into gratefulness, yet he admitted he liked being a victim. He thought this would be hard to release because he was not sure what topics of conversation he could now share with others.

He listed people from his past who contributed to his "nice boy" syndrome and then thanked them. He also forgave himself for wanting to be a people pleaser, thus opening him to accept the joy.

Laughing at the whole scenario he stated, "What a waste of energy."

Later Jack came over and told me his cousin, "Queen Bee," called and apologized. He was able to give her other options for completing her taxes, ones that did not involve him and he was able to do so without using any sarcasm or expressing his ill temper.

With a funny look on his face he asked, "Do you think this really works?"

Shari Lyn's Story

In this next situation you can see how one does not need to do all the steps to get results. The more you use this technique and learn to catch yourself quickly, the easier it is to get to the bottom of your emotional attachment.

Shari Lyn's normal day starts out with exercise, a shower, breakfast and work. After work she runs errands, spends time with her family, reads, and goes to bed.

She started sharing how nice her relationship was with her "was-band" (the phrase she uses for her former husband) and was hoping life could stay this way.

Her daughter, who is 21 and still lives with Shari Lyn, had sided with her father on an issue because the daughter was mad at Shari Lyn. The daughter accused her mom of being just like Shari Lyn's mother. Immediately Shari Lyn moved into the questions.

She asked herself, *Why did that hurt so deeply? What has not been released about my mother? What still haunts me about my mother and what do I still blame my mother for in my life?*

Shari Lyn then realized that she had been trying to make a decision about pursuing her career. If she pursued it, she would not be the perfect mate and mother that her family expected her to be. Like her own mother, she would go her own path and the family would not have her playing the role they desired from her.

She decided she could let go of the belief that she had to choose between her career and her family. She had not made up her mind about her career choice, which made her choosing even more difficult but decided to be truly grateful for everyone involved.

With the accusation from her daughter hurting so deeply and so recently, she wasn't ready to let the joy in yet.

When people short-cut the steps, they will often delay moving to the release and accepting the joy in the last step so they may double-check the incident to see if another layer can be peeled off first. This is appropriate for those who are comfortable with the process and with themselves. This assures them that they are not in denial of any repressed feelings because they want to be complete with this lesson.

While Shari Lyn skips steps, she doesn't miss the lesson, like the story of the following lady.

Trisha's Story

Trisha wakes up at sunrise, feeds the cats and dogs, reads inspirational literature, works on web pages, and takes her shower before going to work. She wears the same style of clothes each day, drives the same route to work, parks in the same spot, pets the dog, punches the time clock, and is ready for a routine day.

While doing routine paperwork and answering the phone, she talks with the bookkeeper in the office. Mostly they talk about the boss and how they could run the business better. Some discussions last longer than others, but they always come to the same conclusion: It is his business and he can run it any way he likes. They are powerless to change it, or him.

She never thinks about having anything new, just tries to stay grateful for what she has in her life.

She says she only sees people who have less than she from the perspective of how she may help them.

Therefore no one ever upsets her, nor does she judge others. If Trisha gets even a little annoyed, she feels she needs more love, so she goes home and gets "one with the universe".

This was the end of the interview, because without wanting to change any unwanted patterns, not wanting anything new in your life, or no uneasy feelings about anything, it's difficult to find a place to start. Does she still have blocks? Sure, and she is willing to live with them. Do they cause her enough pain so she's willing to change them? No. Some people are so removed from their feelings that they really don't feel them anymore. Usually these people give up the good feelings in order to suppress the bad feelings so they stay in a state of no feelings at all.

If you are going to deny that blocks are there, you will not clear them. In a normal day, Trisha had already admitted to judging her boss, making herself align with the bookkeeper by putting someone else down, and making herself a victim by believing there was nothing she could do to change things around her. She also kept herself feeling superior by focusing on others that she judged as having less. Therefore she was out of integrity with herself and thus stifled her own growth.

Integrity is you and your actions aligning or complementing each other. It is also telling yourself the truth, not through rationalization but by being honest about your feelings. It is easy to block or repress unwanted feelings because that is how you have coped with these feeling up until now. You may not be aware that your actions are not consistent with your words or beliefs.

If you listen to what you are really saying when speaking to others, you will learn to hear the difference between what you are saying your life is like and how your life really is. Listening for excuses, explanations, and justifying your actions will help you know that you are out of alignment with what you truly want in your life or what you want your life to look like. If your life looks the way you want it to, there are no excuses.

If you are living as if the unconscious blocks are opportunities to learn, you will have situations in your life that provide an opportunity for you to remove them. You will choose to clear them quickly so you can get on to living the life you want.

If you are living as if the unconscious blocks are boundaries, justifications, or limitations, you will have excuses and reasons why your life looks the way it does.

Noticing that you have to tell people your justifications can be a good wake-up call that your life really isn't how you want it to be.

Two weeks later Trisha told me she was surprised by how many people were upsetting her. This was quite unnerving to her, and she hinted that it was because of our discussion. She had not realized she had been in the "river of De-Nile." Now that she was willing to acknowledge that people were upsetting her, major growth could take place.

The awareness key here is to be aware and take responsibility for your own situations and not blame others for your life circumstances. Look for clues such as blame, justifying and excuses in your life. You are an unlimited being; your accumulation of beliefs is your only limit. Luckily, today on the market there are many tools to help you break down those walls of beliefs, and they are more accessible, acceptable and affordable. Some of these include hypnotic regressions, yoga that involves deep breathing, Reiki, Shamanic Journey work, dousing, body tapping, gong therapy, prayer, meditation, rebirthing, therapeutic grade oils, Awakenings, aromatherapy, color therapy, music or toning therapy, massage and even just continued focused attention, to name a few. Most of the highly effective programs combine more than one of the above-mentioned techniques.

Martha's Story

Martha is a lady who is hardworking, organized and dependable.

She wakes up without an alarm, has her coffee, drinks her protein drink, works out at the gym, runs errands and goes to work. After work, Martha comes home, goes through her mail, watches the news, has a snack, reads, watches television or works on the novel she's writing.

She has in mind that she wants to move to another state, take up residence with a lover and help out a friend who is starting a retreat.

These all have been on her list for a couple of years, and she is still wondering why she has not moved and is not living with Prince Charming.

Then her boss really made her mad by stating they were going to do a big promotion, although he refused to do anything to get ready for it.

Martha slammed around the office for a day or two until she started seeing that she was not gaining anything out of staying mad. However, she did have everyone catering to her wants and desires.

Yet, as in all good things, she decided it truly was not fun anymore. Nothing was really changing; Martha could not stand the agitation or other co-workers avoiding her.

She got a pencil and paper and wrote, "What did my boss's behavior tell me about my boss?" Her list included that her boss was a people pleaser, he liked keeping things in chaos, saving people was a big motivator in his actions and the boss was unwilling to set boundaries around himself emotionally, physically or mentally. These choices in lifestyle for the boss kept the people in the office putting out fires instead of progressing in their work. Then Martha answered the question, "What does that say about me?"

"Because I see what the boss is doing, I become upset and I know that's not healthy. Then I take on responsibility without authority and have a hard time getting others to help, which in turn frustrates me. Also I feel disappointed in my boss for not knowing a better methodology at his age." Martha admitted her life was not what she thought it would be at this point in her life. This brought up the point that Martha is tired of playing the role of mother for her boss. After the interview was over, Martha realized she wished someone would mother her and that she would allow herself to be mothered.

Martha was really glad to let go of this block because she had wanted to change her behavior for years.

She frantically started her list of people to be grateful for, including her mom for teaching her Prince Charming would be the only one with the power to change her life. Martha could see she no longer had to depend on a Prince Charming to change her life. She was capable of making changes to her life all by herself. Martha then forgave herself and everyone else for how they had played their role.

She could release quickly all those fairy tales that she believed as truths and let the joy fill her heart. Martha was still laughing as she walked out the door saying, "I probably make my boss nuts because of how I do things, just like he makes me nuts."

Lisa's Story

Lisa is a lovely woman with a jolly laugh and a smile that would light up a windowless room.

Her typical day starts with a morning thank you to God for life. Then she acknowledges the birds and nature. She also says her prayer to "aid me in being the best me, light person, true friend and blessing to the world while remembering God's presence and trusting that God is in charge." She prays for her loved ones and friends, world leaders, peace to the world and all people before she has breakfast, showers and dresses for the day. Then Lisa is on her way.

She runs errands, hers and her friends', and goes to her office where she works with clients, does paper work and makes phone calls. After work, Lisa exercises, takes walks and goes to group gatherings.

One day Lisa was reflecting on her life by taking an inventory. She realized that her life was small and limited.

She started thinking about the people that she notices living an expanded lifestyle and wondered why she was not one of those neat people.

That day the 77-year-young woman who serves as her landlady, mentor, and confidant, started imposing household and time limits on Lisa, as well as criticizing Lisa's actions. Lisa started feeling like she could do nothing right. She was criticized for taking walks, having her door closed, not being around enough, which made her feel like giving up, wanting to go her separate way, and moving out of the house so she could avoid the whole situation.

The landlady then asked her to find another place to live.

Lisa quickly felt like processing all of this so she came to me and asked for assistance. My first question was: What actually happened and where else in your life did that occur? Lisa felt the same restraints she had felt when she lived at home with her parents. She was experiencing the same fear of losing everything if she dared to do the things she wanted or if she created any boundaries for herself personally. Lisa felt that if she took this road of expanding her world, she would lose friends, family and her basic survival comforts like food, clothing and shelter.

She saw that this was an old pattern. Obviously she created it because it had happened many times with others.

When I asked if she was ready to grow past this, she replied, "Please!"

We listed everyone involved in this play and all the people in all the other plays where this same pattern occurred. This included friends, family members, landlords and children. After forgiving herself and all the people she had named, she forgave everyone into infinity. This forgiveness was important for her, and she felt it released her from the mindset of the here and now.

As she finished, her hands flew into the air and she said, "I will have to play with this." She was singing as she made her way to her car.

Boni's Story

I was born the fourth girl on a small farm in rural Pennsylvania to a father who taught biology in the local high school and a mother who put her teaching career on hold to raise her children. When I was five my brother was born.

We had horses and ponies, chickens, sheep, a dog and cats. My older sister was known to take in strays, so we always had neighbors that gave us a cow or a pig that was the runt of the litter.

My dad was always being called on to retrieve squirrels from attics or to identify fish that were caught in the river. My parents were related to just about everyone in the town of four hundred people where we went to school and also in the neighboring towns that were even smaller.

Money was rare in my life, and it didn't seem to matter as my mom grew our food and canned everything. We picked apples and all types of berries, which she made into pies and sauces. In her spare time she made our clothes. We bought milk from the couple who had dairy cows and eggs from the lady who always had extra.

We were okay financially because of my dad teaching high school. He was also the Justice of the Peace, and he farmed, so we even got to travel. We went anywhere my dad heard was a good fishing spot, and, because he was a history buff, we saw every single battlefield and fort.

On summer holidays we got together with four generations of relatives for picnics at the pond on the family farm where my uncle's family lived. We swam, fished, played baseball and ate pot luck with grandparents, aunts, uncles, cousins, and any friends that were invited.

As wonderful as this all sounds, I still had a lot of confusion growing up. I never knew who I was or where I fit in. My oldest sister was the farmer, the next sister was the smart one, and the sister just a year older than I could get any boy she wanted. I thought of myself as never being good enough because I wasn't the boy my dad had hoped for.

It was tough thinking of me as a failure about something I could do nothing about so I just quit trying to please everyone. Anything I did seemed to make someone unhappy. It made me curious how some people could have anything they wanted and were happy all the time, and I couldn't do anything without getting into trouble. I decided I had to find out why, because I was told we were all the same, so why didn't I feel the same?

I wanted it all. I wanted a closer relationship with my husband, better working environment, children, extra money, friends, peace of mind, joy, happiness, freedom and the ability to help other people.

I wanted to give up worrying, hearing people's problems, just making enough money each month to get by, and feeling frustrated with my life in general.

When I first learned about this system of clearing unwanted beliefs that were blocking what I wanted from coming into my life, I didn't believe it would work, but I was willing to try anything at that point.

The first thing I did was write down everything that I wanted in my life. This list was made up of 257 things, feelings, and relationships. I put this list in an envelope and sealed it.

Then I made a list of 10 things that if I had them in my life would make my life easier.

From that list, I picked one thing to focus on continuously. Focusing on this one thing brought up all the unspoken beliefs I had adopted as a child.

It brought up memories of how I had to take what was left after the older sisters got what they needed. It brought up shameful feelings that if I thought of myself above their needs, I was being selfish.

So my life consisted of trying to live everyone else's life, thinking of what they needed, and seeing other people happy so then I could do for me. My new realization was I could decide what I wanted.

By this time I was married, and I was helping my husband with his pottery business. I worked as a bookkeeper, and then quit to go to college to become a computer programmer.

We had bought a house so we could set up a kiln. I was working in the garage glazing the pottery, and we did craft shows to sell the wares.

We thought about how it would be easier to have a place where we could just turn on the lights instead of packing the pottery, making and hauling displays, driving to the show, unpacking, spend two days selling, and then packing everything back up and hauling it home.

We made our list of what we wanted, and then turned it into a story or movie script. We imagined what it would be like to have a shop where we could demonstrate the making of the pottery, talk to people from all over the world, sell our pottery, and be in a place with beautiful surroundings accompanied by other artists who would be willing to share ideas and strategies about marketing and product development. This became our new focus.

My husband, Doug, also taught people to make pottery on the potter's wheel, and one of his students suggested we might be interested in selling him pottery wholesale for his candle business. This student also had a small shop in a complex of artists that might be interested in having a potter.

We did both and in a few months we had opened a retail store where Doug could demonstrate and sell pottery. I was just finishing computer programming school and because running the shop, making the pottery and keeping up with the wholesale orders was more than Doug could do by himself; I went to work for him.

In cleaning out the store one day, I came across our original list of what we wanted in the shop. Everything we asked for was on that list. Reviewing it, we made a few changes. Instead of just being in beautiful surroundings, we wanted to be able to see them so we included a window. Two years later our son was born, and we had expanded the shop to include the window. As a bonus we could see through to the outside and the beautiful surroundings.

We met people from all over the world, some of whom didn't speak English. The other craftsmen were wonderful and shared with us ways to make taking custom orders easier. An added benefit was that they had lots of ideas of what other things we could make to sell.

With the potter's wheel set up and Doug making things, people easily saw what it took to make the pottery and asked about classes. It took a couple of years, but we expanded the shop to include classes.

We both wanted to stay home and care for our son. We hired help to sell in the retail store, Doug made pottery in a room in the house, and I continued to glaze and fire the pottery at home.

By now I was also really jazzed that I could have my life the way I wanted plus we were managing a store, employees, government paperwork, and wanting to raise our son without our limited mindset, so I listened to recordings while I glazed. I took as many classes as I could to understand why this system of focused attention and clearing blocks worked.

Silva Mind control was out in paperback so I read it and did the exercises, then signed up for the class. Other classes on relationships became available through the Natale Institute, so Doug and I both went. From there we got interested in shamanic journeying from tapes by Ed Gross. I continually took classes and taught what I had learned to enhance my understanding and to share with others ways to make their lives easier, too. The following are some of the classes, workshops and lectures I attended: Silva Mind control, Inner Peace movement, Christ Singh, Sri Siva, Anthony Robbins, The Natale Institute series, Yogi Bhajan, Course in Miracles tapes, Akashic Record consulting, Shamanic Journeying, Hypnosis, Raymon Grace dowsing, Awakenings, Access, Numerology, Reiki, Dr. Dan's network chiropractic, handwriting analysis, sacred geometry, the art of visioneering, dream interpretation, Sai Baba's teaching, Shai Babaji's way of life, Jean

Houston workshops, Feng Shui, Neimology, body tapping, and Dr. David Hawkins' lectures.

I was really intrigued with this whole new world and way of thinking. We combined some pottery and shamanic journeying as a unique experience. Then, after getting certified as a hypnotherapist, I started teaching a six-week class combining much of what I had learned.

Life was good but I wanted an air conditioned environment in which to work. So I pictured every morning and every night before going to bed what it would look like and feel like to be in such an environment.

Before long I got the idea to think bigger. So I included the surroundings around which my air conditioned work area would be. Again we made a list of everything that would be included, such as the view, community, and school for our son. This we sealed away in another envelope.

We spent one afternoon driving to small communities. The cost of what I pictured was way out of our price range, but instead of giving up, we got the idea to run an ad in the community paper asking if anyone had three-to-five acres where we could build a home and studio.

I received a call from a lady realtor in which she said she had a listing for a 3.25-acre tract of land on a hillside. This property wasn't much to look at because it had been stripped of the rock for use on a road. Also it had been part of a small farm in which this listing was used as the dumping ground.

Because of the bad shape the land was in, it had a sale price of $13,500 and didn't include water well, electric or septic.

This was affordable, so we checked to make sure we could acquire the needed well, electric and septic, and that it could be built upon as well as a road put in.

We bought the property. We used all our savings putting in the basic electric, well and septic, and then started looking for a builder.

We found a builder who would do the framing and who sectioned off a part for us to live in so we could put our house in town up for sale.

No one seemed interested in our old house by the time we were ready to move into our bare-necessity frame of a house, so we offered owner financing. The realtor suggested a wraparound note, which kept the house and payment in our name while the new owners took possession, thus allowing us to move in two weeks.

We had only a concrete floor, a kitchen sink held up with two by fours, a toilet, and tub in 700 square feet in which to create a home. The pottery studio we wanted could not be built because we couldn't afford to borrow any more money. We were now making payments on the old house and the new place. But we had 1000 square feet of the house that needed insulation, sheet rock, plumbing, flooring, and wiring so that we could use it for a studio.

Throughout this time we constantly envisioned the place completed, including air conditioning. We would laugh as we were sweating, telling each other how great it felt to be in our 1000-square-foot studio with hot and cold running water, cool air blowing on us, and a real floor.

Wonderful things happened and wonderful people showed up to assist us. Materials showed up at a fraction of the cost first bid to us; relatives bought us gifts of bathroom sinks, toilet, and a shower. One couple even used their vacation time to install insulation, sheet rock and wiring. It was three years before we could put in flooring.

We looked at our original list that we had created, and there were a few things different from the reality of our home and studio. The view we wanted out the back was out the front, and we had a bonus of a beautiful starry sky at night. We not only got great neighbors but they had a son almost the same age as our son.

By focused thought and removing the blocks that arose, I was able to build a building to continue to teach classes and host other teachers. Eventually, through the generosity of people and divine timing, we built the pottery workshop we wanted and reclaimed our house for a home. All the while we lived the life we wanted by volunteering at a local church, my husband's organizations, and my son's school and scouts' groups.

People continually opened doors for me and gifted me with their friendships, advice and acquaintances for which I am eternally grateful. I received Certification in Akashic Record Consultation, then Teaching with Akashic Record Consultants International.

I would like to share with you some of the people and classes I took as I feel very fortunate to have received classes from the founders as well as from their apprentices. I apologize to anyone I forgot on this list as it has been a 30-year journey so far. Remember also that these were *my* experiences, and what I needed to learn at the time of my unfolding. They may not be for you, and not all of them are still available. I believe in divine guidance and know your divinity will guide you as mine has guided me.

- Meeting people like *Jose Siva* and knowing his sincerity about what he believed people could do with their minds expanded my mind.
- *Inner Peace* movement was started by *Francisco Cole* because of his ability to talk to and interpret an angel's touch on his body. He taught me to use my body as an instrument to receive answers from the angelic world, interoperating my body movements to understand yes and no answers to my questions. They also create goose flesh, or goose bumps, on various parts of the body to convey direction, truth, or guidance.
- *Christ Singh's* teachings on the mysticism of Christ gave me a whole new look at Christianity. This allowed me to open my heart to the Christianity I grew up with but didn't understand.
- *Sri Siva* course put me in tune with the sounds of the universe that put me back into alignment with my true self.
- *Anthony Robbins'* course was a valuable tool for awareness in effective communication with me and others in life and business.
- The *Natale Institute* is Frank Natale's creation, and although I didn't know him well, he was the most compassionate man I ever met. His understanding of the human physic and how he communicates it through his workshops have had a huge impact in my life. His courses, still in their original form taught by Wilbert Alix, have evolved to include Trance dancing.
- *Yogi Bhajan's gong therapy* is just wild. Listening or meditating to sounds from that giant gong not only released old beliefs but also brought up questions for me to make choices in my life using only vibrations.
- The *Course in Miracles* is considered a spiral way of learning. It is mental but it is also experiential as the examples in the written material will surface in my life.
- The *Akashic Record* classes really hit home for me. I felt like I was home the first time I opened my records. Learning was fast with the easy direct way I was taught to connect to the energy of my own records. It has been so powerful for me that I became a Certified Consultant and then a Certified Teacher with Akashic Record Consultants International. There is no

describing the unlimited growth that has taken place for me by this resource and it continues to do so. This also let me help others in ways that I could only dream about before.

- *Shamanic journey* work has been fun for me because it transcends the logical mind into a world of symbolism and knowing. Therefore, it is hard to completely describe in words to others the amount of completion that takes place. This started for me by listening to tapes by Ed Gross and Sandra Ingerman then moving into experimentation with many teachers including Frank Natale, Masauki, and Hal.

- Hypnosis gave me some really good guidelines to follow as well as some understanding of why some things work long term and why some things work only short term. My best results were with the regressions as they took me to the place where the very first situation happened and allowed me to change the original experience. With the root experience changed, it changed behaviors and old unwanted feelings in my life.

- Understanding and using *Raymon Grace's* dowsing techniques are the foundation I use to measure and convert energy quickly. He taught me to understand and play with energy using his dowsing techniques, measure the results I got, and expand my limited thinking. He is constantly relooking at how and why he approaches the subject the way he does. This allows him or anyone else using this system to find short-cuts or more effective ways to receive wanted results.

- *An awakening,* as instructed and performed by Ron Hall, is brought forth from his gift of clear ability to directly communicate with guides from the spirit world. These awakenings included surgery in the energetic body of a person to remove blocks of stuck energy. I have been fortunate to work with his apprentices Lucy Destin and Glenda Garber.

- Although *Access* has been around for thousands of years, Gary Douglass reawakened it. He taught me to use my energy to follow energy back to the original block, confusion, or point of creation, then discharge the energy that locks it in, neutralizing the effect it has in my life.

- Meanwhile I read a lot of books, listened to tapes and watched videos or DVDs. Napoleon Hill's *Think and Grow Rich* book was top on the list. *Ramtha* gave me some keys to look at myself by who I blamed or gave power too. *Shad Helmstetter* let me look at how I repeatedly talked to myself. Earl Nightingall's *The Strangest Secret*, as well as his continual series, hosting many wonderful speakers, was all great and invaluable in my life.
- Classes and consultations with the *Lightkeepers* through Sharon Wythe helped me to keep things in perspective.
- *Numerology* helped me better understand stronger tendencies of how I view life.
- *Reiki* was a pure energy release for me that allowed stuck energy to move without having to be consciously aware of what caused the block or having to relive it.
- *Dr. Dan* is a networking chiropractor. He muscle tests by moving the feet so that the clearing is cellular. His work is painless and has allowed me to own some of things I have learned.
- *Handwriting analysis* gave me insight into hidden character beliefs about myself and others. This continues to be helpful as a way to understand people and their main objectives.
- *Sacred geometry* let me reset the structure of the energy field, which eventually resets the physical. Understanding the alignment and structure of energy put into perspective the building of my life.
- The art of *visioneering* really focused me on how to visualize.
- *Dream interpretation* allowed me to view my life symbolically.
- *Sai Baba's* teaching and *Shai Babaji* philosophy assisted in simplifying my life.
- *Jean Houston* workshops were fun as well as revealing inner conflicts.
- Stacy Davenport's *Paradigm Shift* and *Feng Shui* used to enhance the flow of energy in my home.
- *Neimology* helped me understand other people's soul mission through the letters in their names.

- *Body tapping, Dr. David Hawkins'* lectures, *Matrix Entergenics*, and others added to my understanding of me, different cultures and clearing of unwanted beliefs.

The basics were all the same:

Know where you are, know what you want, visualize what you want, listen to your inner guidance, collect resources, do the first steps to create what you want, see what shows up in your life, make corrections, clear or change your beliefs, continue to hold the picture of what you want, notice how the physical world looks and reinvent how you see yourself. Remember that you can only change you and how you interoperate with the world around you.

How all the presenters of their system went about finding what people wanted and how they proceeded to change the beliefs were different processes. Some worked faster than others for me but they all worked to some degree.

CHAPTER 7

True Freedom

The secret of happiness is freedom. The secret of freedom
is courage.—Thucydides

True Freedom

True Freedom widens your path. Your path is where you can walk, the people you can meet and the experiences you can have with comfort.

When you first start down your path, it is very narrow because the comfort of your experiences is based on the first seven years of your life. This is where you learned what is acceptable in the world around you, what is allowed and what is proper.

By clearing the conclusions you came to as a child and the disempowering conditioning you received at this time in your life, your path widens to allow more choices, therefore you get to decide what is right for you. The beliefs that people gave you about what is right, proper or acceptable may have worked for them but may not be what is working for you now in creating the life you want.

It's much like clearing the minefields at the edges of your path. The mine fields are the hurt, frustration and anger that result in stepping in a new direction as you make your way through life. With the path cleared of these unpleasant feelings erupting from time to time, you have many more chances of choosing with each step you take. Really getting clear of these eruptions allows you to get clarity about what you want your life to look like without guilt, nagging thoughts and feelings of regret.

Knowing what you want, asking for what you want, knowing you have the right to choose what you want and living the life you want from choice is true freedom. It is time now for you to get on with your life and your choices. Please accept my blessings to all of you who have the courage and strength to change consciously because "the only constant in the universe is change."

MY STORY
from and by Glenda Garber and the Record Keepers
(as received in Akashic Records Level 3 class)

I was born into a family made up of all muggles
So I could experience lots and lots of hard struggles
My life was confusing, which they all found amusing
The more I protested my lot, the worser and worser it got.

I did it this way many years and a day until finally I said "enough."
And I started to search for the truth of my birth.
Here I would find more powerful minds to help me let go of my stuff.

I went to the counselors, I read all the books,
I went to the priests—and the workshops I took!!!!!
I found many truths, many spiritual paths
And I learned "less is more" and "the first shall be last."

But the answers I sought after, so hard and so long
Always seemed to evade me though my desires were strong
Frustration was building ... "Where at all had I gone?"

Until at last I felt—only one more place to go
If this didn't work, I'd have nothing to show.
I went to my heart, my very own self
And there I found answers that fit me the best
It was then I was able to let go of the rest
And come into my own with my great higher self.

Now things are different, I know who I am
Things that work for me now just didn't work then
The difference I tell you is the work that I've done,
The play and the process and the bundles of fun.

A new family for sure, I've created quite nicely
From all over the country, they call to be with me.
And we come to Skye Island to play and have fun
The how-to's and schedules, we let the keepers run.
We play in the energies and make up new games
We sing and we dance and we laugh when it rains.

When zings come to surface to disturb our sweet peace
We have prayer cards and releases and grace points for each.
We have Awakenings, labyrinths and dance ceremonies too
When Faye is around, who knows when we'll be through?

The journey is endless with treasures galore
And the guidance says, "Oh, there is more, more and more."
So on we all go, in our most happy way,
Knowing that all is accomplished with nothing but play.
The joy that comes to me fills every cell
It's a feeling that, somewhere, I've always known quite well.
Thanks ya'll!

Boni Oian is a Certified Akashic Record
Teacher and Consultant, Hypnotist, and
Director of All Encompassing Retreats
www.TransformationalReAlignment.com,
www.AllEncompassingRetreats.com,
www.AkashicRecordsTraining.com,
www.SunrisePottery.com
www.ClaimYourLifewithBoni.com

Emily Sanderson is a writer, counselor, and life coach in San
Antonio, Texas www.EmilySanderson.com

CPSIA information can be obtained at www.ICGtesting.com
Printed in the USA
LVOW120100031111

253257LV00001B/7/P